PUFFIN BOOKS

SCIENCE IS LIT

AWESOME ELECTRICITY AND MAD MAGNETS

PUFFIN BOOKS

UK | USA | Canada | Ireland | Australia
India | New Zealand | South Africa

Penguin Books is part of the Penguin Random House group of companies
whose addresses can be found at global.penguinrandomhouse.com.

www.penguin.co.uk
www.puffin.co.uk
www.ladybird.co.uk

Penguin
Random House
UK

First published 2025

001

Text copyright © Emanuel Wallace, 2025
Illustration copyright © Subi Bosa, 2025

The moral right of the author and illustrator has been asserted

Printed at Thomson Press India Ltd, New Delhi

The authorized representative in the EEA is Penguin Random House Ireland,
Morrison Chambers, 32 Nassau Street, Dublin D02 YH68

A CIP catalogue record for this book is available from the British Library

ISBN: 978-0-241-65383-8

All correspondence to:
Puffin Books
Penguin Random House Children's
One Embassy Gardens, 8 Viaduct Gardens, London SW11 7BW

BIG MANNY

SCIENCE IS LIT

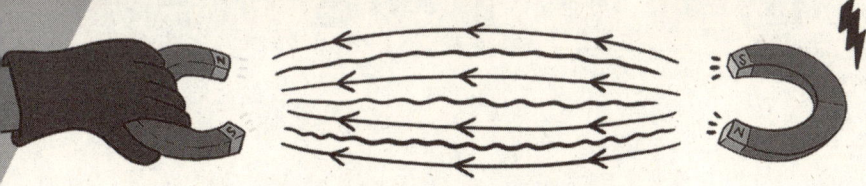

AWESOME ELECTRICITY AND MAD MAGNETS

ILLUSTRATED BY
SUBI BOSA

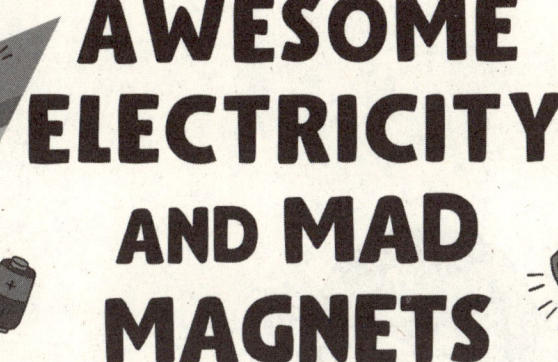

PUFFIN

CONTENTS

HI, I'M EMANUEL – BUT YOU MIGHT KNOW ME AS BIG MANNY.

I'm a scientist who does explosive experiments and crazy science on TikTok. Sometimes I do these experiments in front of a live audience or even on TV! And in this book, I'm going to teach you how to do your own experiments at home and become a real-life scientist, **INIT.**

I was a very curious kid, and growing up, I had loads of questions. Science always fascinated me because it taught me about the real world – the things I can see, feel, touch, hear and taste.

INTRODUCTION

Like, say, the pull I feel when I bring two magnets close together. **How can these magnets pull together but I can't see anything pulling them?** That's mad.

Or the rainbows I see after it rains – **where do those colours come from**?

And **why does my shadow copy everything I do**?

Science gave me the answers to these questions. But learning the answers only led me to ask even more questions! So I decided to study science at university and got two degrees in biomedical science. After I graduated, I worked in a school as a science technician.

PHYSICS TING

In this book, we're gonna learn all about **PHYSICS**. Physics is all around us – we can see it in everything we do, and I mean that literally because for us to see, we need light. Light **reflects** – or bounces back – off objects and enters our eyes. And the study of light is part of physics.

DONE KNOW.

So what is physics? OK, so first, I need to introduce you to a new word. This word is **matter**. Now, everything in the world is made up of either one of two things: **physical matter** or **energy**. You're made of matter, as is this book, and even the trees and buildings you see around you.

Physical matter is things like **solids**, **liquids** and **gases**. So everything that you can see, touch and feel is physical matter.

Energy is stuff that we can't touch – or sometimes even see – but it's still there. **Sound** is an example of energy. We can't see sound, but we can definitely hear it, and feel it too!

Another example of energy is **magnetism**. We can't actually see a magnetic force pulling two metals together, but we can feel it.

INTRODUCTION

Even mobile phones use energy matter. Every time a phone call is made, **radio waves** travel from a mobile-phone mast to the mobile phone itself. These radio waves are invisible to the human eye, but there are millions of them travelling through the air every single second!

Physical matter is made up of **atoms**. But **what is an atom**? An atom is one of the smallest things in the entire universe. If you zoomed in on anything super closely, you would eventually see atoms. Atoms are one of the things to make up physical matter. And when you join two or more atoms together, it makes a **molecule**. An example of a molecule is water – a water molecule is made up of two hydrogen atoms and one oxygen.

LOADS OF WATER MOLECULES GROUP TOGETHER TO FORM THE FLOWING WATER THAT WE LOVE TO DRINK.

Right, to explain this, imagine I took your hand and placed it under a microscope, then began to zoom in. First, we'll see the tiny hairs on your skin, then as we zoom in a bit more, we'll see the likkle holes that these hairs grow from (these are called pores). Let's zoom in a bit more, and we'll see the individual cells that make up your skin. If we zoom in on those cells, we'll see some DNA – the genetic code that controls things like whether you have blue or brown eyes, straight or curly hair. DNA is made up of atoms.

On the other hand, energy – such as sound and light – is not made of atoms. Instead, energy is made of waves. We can't actually touch these waves, but we can see and feel their effects in the world.

To prove this, grab a container, go outside and try to capture a piece of sunlight in the container. You just can't do it – it's impossible! **We can't touch light because it's not a physical object, but we can feel the warmth that comes from the Sun's rays. Sound isn't a physical object, so we can't touch that either.** The same goes for the radio waves from a mobile phone.

THE ELECTROMAGNETIC SPECTRUM

Let's take a closer look at this energy that moves in waves. There's bare different types of waves – there's a whole spectrum! This spectrum is called the **electromagnetic spectrum**, and it includes those light waves and radio waves that we spoke about.

Not all waves are the same – some are long, whereas others are short. For example, radio waves can be hundreds of miles long! But light waves are really short – less than 1 millimetre (mm) long.

We use different waves for different purposes. **There are seven different types of waves on the electromagnetic spectrum**, and I've listed them here from longest to shortest:

★ **RADIO WAVES:** Mobile phones, TV and radio stations all use radio waves to send messages, calls or programmes from one place to another.

★ **MICROWAVES:** Microwave ovens use microwaves to heat up food! The waves travel into your food and cook it from the inside. Mad ting.

★ **INFRARED RAYS:** These are used in remote controls, thermometers and barcode scanners. If you see that red light that comes from a barcode scanner – that's infrared!

★ **VISIBLE LIGHT:** Clue's in the name, fam! This is the light our eyes actually process! Visible light includes natural light from the Sun, and artificial or man-made light such as light from lightbulbs. Cameras and telescopes use visible light in order to capture images and magnify them (make them bigger).

★ **ULTRAVIOLET (OR UV) LIGHT:** Now, ultraviolet (or UV) light is kinda special. Have you ever seen one of those invisible-ink pens where you need a special purple light for the ink to show up? That's UV light, and it makes the ink become visible because the ink contains special substances that can only be seen under this type of light. That's how you can write secret messages and that!

★ **X-RAYS:** Have you ever had an X-ray? This is when doctors take pictures of your bones – it's a mad ting. X-rays are so powerful that they can travel through your skin and muscles, but not through your bones, which is why bones show up as white shadows and help the doctors work out what might be going on with you. Crazy stuff.

★ **GAMMA RAYS**: These are even more powerful than X-rays, and doctors can also use these to take images of the body.

MEET THE MAIN CHARACTERS

OK, so in this book, we're gonna get to know some different types of energy – let's call them our main characters.

One of the characters we're gonna meet is **ELECTRICITY**. Electricity is super charged up – I'll be honest, it's a bit of a prankster and loves to shock you! You don't really wanna mess with electricity because it's bare powerful. Electricity powers all our household electrical appliances such as fridges, kettles, ovens and more.

Next up we have **LIGHT**. Now light is really friendly and light-hearted, and loves to make people laugh with funny jokes. Light is also a key character because without light, we would all be in darkness! Our eyes need light to be able to see.

We're also going to meet the marvellous **MAGNET**. Now magnet has got real superpowers – it can attract anything it wants without lifting a finger. Once magnet attracts something, it's hard to escape its pull. You can normally find magnet chilling out on the fridge door.

Lastly, we have **SOUND**. Now sound just loves to vibe and play music. I can't lie; sound can be a bit loud sometimes, but overall it's pretty cool. You can catch it in the music studio with the piano and drums.

EXPERIMENT TIME

Now that we know what physics is all about, it's time to get experimenting. Before we do, I'm gonna need you to watch out for a few things. You'll notice each experiment has a difficulty rating, from **SIMPLE TING** (easy), to **COME ON NOW** (medium) and **BIG SCIENCE** (advanced). The **SIMPLE TING** experiments are designed to be easy enough for you to do them by yourself. If I say **COME ON NOW**, you may need an adult to help you, so ask an adult to be present. And when we get to **BIG SCIENCE**, this is proper advanced science, so defo ask an adult to help you and don't try these alone!

DIFFICULTY LEVEL:
Simple Ting

DIFFICULTY LEVEL:
Come On Now

DIFFICULTY LEVEL:
Big Science

To give you a bit of a head start, sometimes I've added results from me, but other times I've left you to fill in your own.

A few of the experiments can also get a bit messy! Wherever you see the splat symbol, make sure you get an adult to help you with the experiment, and with cleaning up afterwards.

As well as scientific experiments, this book is full of scientific facts and knowledge – some of it is real easy, but some of it is bare challenging to help you **LEVEL UP** your science game. Where you see the level-up symbol, it means this is the tricky stuff, so have a go if you want to challenge yourself – but if you want to skip it and just try the experiment, that's cool too.

If you don't know what some words mean, there's also a glossary on p.199 to help you.

HOW TO BE SAFE

Ite cool, safety is bare important still, I can't lie. Before we do any experiments, here are some important steps to follow:

★ Scientists always wear goggles to protect our eyes when we're doing experiments. Goggles make sure that no liquids splash into our eyes and hurt us. If you don't have lab goggles at home, swimming goggles also work fine for home experiments!

★ For static electricity experiments, make sure your hands are completely dry. Keep electronics and flammable materials away from static electricity experiments.

★ Whenever we are doing an experiment, we should always be standing up. If something spills, it's easier to move out of the way if we are standing up instead of sitting down. (If you are a wheelchair user or if standing for periods of time might be hard for you, speak to your adult to work out the best way to conduct the experiment safely together.)

★ If you have any pets, or younger brothers or sisters, make sure they're safely out of the way!

★ Make sure to dispose of any mixtures safely. If you're not sure of the best way to do this, ask a grown-up for their advice. And remember to clear up any mess afterwards!

★ When using liquids, put down some newspaper or old tea towels on your work surface and floor – in case things get messy. And always wash your hands after experiments.

★ If anything does splash into your eyes or on to your skin, wash with plenty of cold water.

★ Another safety rule is not eating or drinking when we are doing an experiment. This is to make sure that any chemicals that we are using don't get into our food.

★ Always handle batteries and magnets safely and with extra care, and ask an adult for help.

★ Lastly, never run around while doing an experiment as we wouldn't want to knock any chemicals or equipment over.

BOOM! Now that we know how to be safe and that, let's get started on our first chapter – how to be a scientist!

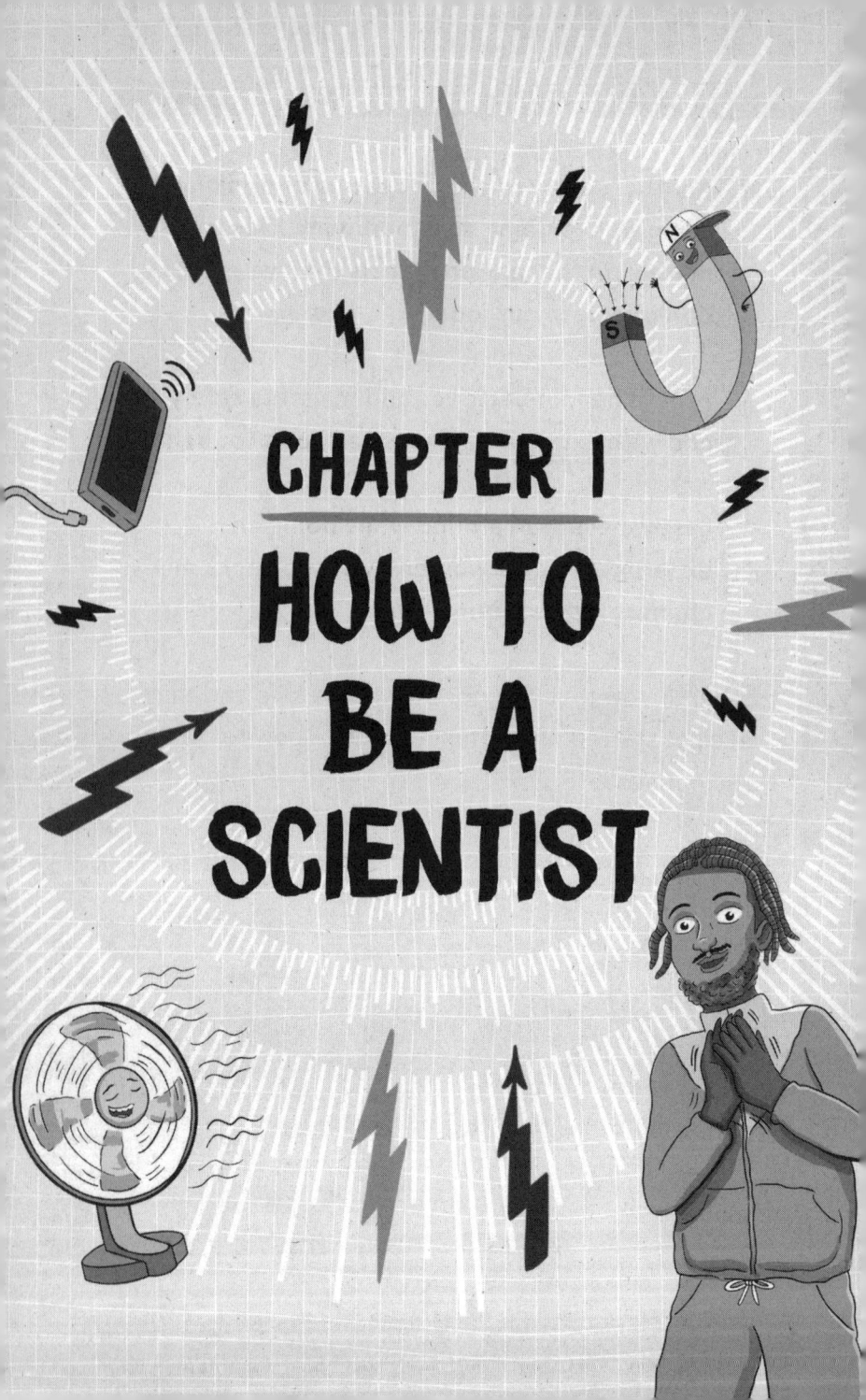

CHAPTER 1

HOW TO
BE A
SCIENTIST

OK, before we get started on some experiments, yeah, I'm gonna run you through some of the key things you need to be a real scientist. Now before we start any experiment, there are seven main things we need to think about. These are:

1. Experiment aim
First we need to know what our aim is. **The aim of an experiment is what you're trying to find out.** Another way you can think of this is, what question are you trying to answer? For example, let's say we had a range of different objects, and we wanted to find out whether they float or sink when placed in water. The aim of the experiment would simply be to investigate whether different objects float or sink in water. Easy ting!

2. Hypothesis
The second thing we need for an experiment is a hypothesis. **Now, a hypothesis is basically what you think will happen in the experiment.** Or in other words, your prediction. So let's say the objects we have for our experiment are some polystyrene, a stone and a cork. Each one will be put in water to see if it sinks or floats, and I think the polystyrene and cork will float but the stone will sink. That's our hypothesis sorted. Done know.

3. Equipment list

The third thing we need is an equipment list, init. This is literally just **the things we need to do the experiment**. So for this experiment we'll need a bowl, some water and the objects we're testing.

Our equipment list might look like this:
★ large bowl
★ 500ml water
★ piece of polystyrene
★ piece of cork
★ small stone

4. Method

The fourth part of the experiment is the method. The method is **a set of instructions that tell you how to do the experiment**. So for this experiment, we'd need to place the first object in the bowl of water and see whether it sinks or floats. Then, we'd repeat it for the other objects and observe what happens. You get me?

5. Results

For the fifth part, we get the results! Results are basically **what happened in the experiment, or**

the outcome. So for this experiment, we would write down whether each object sank or floated in the water. The stone sank, whereas the polystyrene and cork both floated.

6. Conclusion

The sixth part is the conclusion. For the conclusion, we just have to say **what our results mean**. A more scientific way of saying this is that we are **interpreting the results**. We know that the stone sunk, but what does that tell us? Well, it tells us that the stone has greater density than the water. Density is the measurement of how many atoms are packed into a given space. Objects that are less dense than water will float, but objects that are denser will sink. The polystyrene and cork floated, which means they're less dense than the water.

7. Evaluation

The seventh and final part of an experiment is called the evaluation. This is where we **list the things about the experiment that went well, and things we could do to improve it for next time**. One thing that went well in this experiment is that we used more than one object, which allowed us to compare the density of different substances. To improve it, we could measure how much the water rises when we put the object into it. This would give us more information on its density.

For each of the experiments in the book, we're gonna tick off each of these seven steps. That's how man becomes a proper scientist!

BOOM! EVALUATION DONE.

WHAT ARE VARIABLES?

All scientific experiments have variables. Now, there are three main types of variable:

★ The thing we change in an experiment is called the **INDEPENDENT VARIABLE**.

★ The thing we measure in an experiment is called the **DEPENDENT VARIABLE**.

★ The thing we keep the same is called the **CONTROL**.

So if we go back to our density experiment, the independent variable that changes is the type of object. We're using three different objects –

polystyrene, a stone and a piece of cork – so this variable changes. The dependent variable we're measuring is whether the objects sink or floats. The variable we're keeping the same – or the control – is the amount of water, so we need to make sure we're using the same amount of water for each object.

In experiments, it's bare important that only one variable is changed and one variable is measured. The only thing we're changing is the type of object, and the only thing we're measuring is whether the object floats or sinks. The control – in this case, the amount of water – needs to be kept the same, otherwise it could affect our results and make them **INVALID**. Invalid just means the results of your experiment aren't right, either because of incorrect information or because they can't be repeated. Why do we need to repeat our results though?

ACCURATE VERSUS PRECISE

To be proper scientists, we need to repeat our experiments to make sure we get similar results each time – that way we know our results weren't just a fluke! **If all of our results are similar to each other, it means our results are precise.** But just because the results are precise, it doesn't always mean they are accurate. Accuracy basically means **how close your results are to the correct answer**. You might get a bunch of results that are all similar, meaning they're precise, but they might not be that close to the actual correct answer, meaning they're not accurate. You can make your results more accurate by using exact measurements – for example, in our density experiment we could use a ruler to measure the water before and after we dropped the objects into it. That's how we make sure our results are certified.

HOW TO PRESENT YOUR RESULTS

What we're going to do now is go into a likkle bit more detail about the results part of the experiment. Another word for results is **DATA**. We can present our results – or data – in a few different ways to make the information as clear and easy to understand as possible.

BAR CHARTS

Let's say we're doing an experiment that aims to investigate the eye colours of different students in a class. We count the number of students with each eye colour, and the results are that twenty-one students have brown eyes, seven have blue and two have green. To make the data a bit easier to understand, we can slap it into a table like this:

EYE COLOUR	NUMBER OF STUDENTS
BROWN	21
BLUE	7
GREEN	2

This set of data can also be shown in a bar chart like the one on the next page, init. Bar charts are used for data that has whole numbers, which we call **DiSCRETE DATA**. Each bar represents a different eye colour, and the numbers along the side represent the number of students. If you trace your finger from the top of a bar to the column of numbers on the left-hand side – which we call the Y axis – then you can find out how many students have that eye colour. The row along the bottom (where the eye colours are shown) is called the X axis.

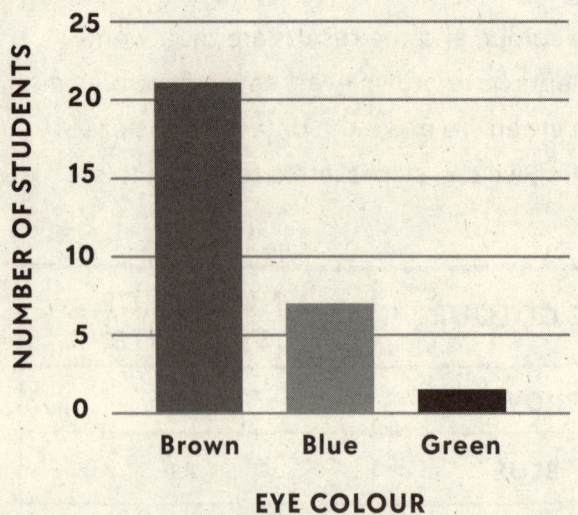

The data in bar charts can be presented in any order and it can still be understood and interpreted correctly. We could put the brown, blue or green bar first and the chart would still make sense. These types of results can also be shown in a **pie chart**.

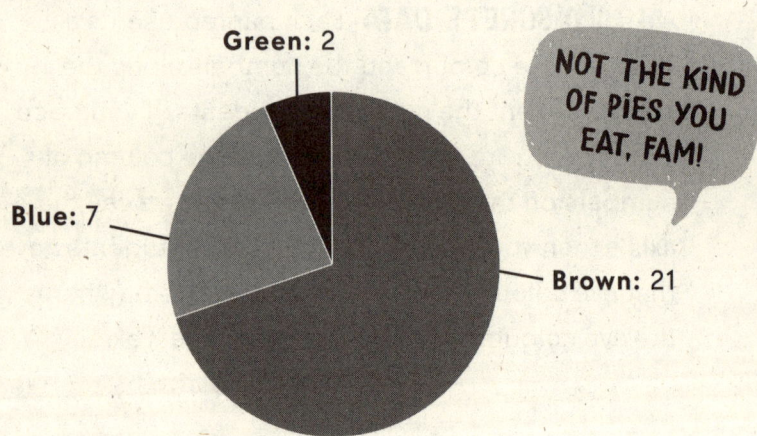

LINE GRAPHS

Another type of graph that we can use to present data is a line graph. Now, line graphs aren't used for discrete data or whole numbers – they're used for **CONTINUOUS DATA**, which means the results are not in whole numbers. An example of continuous data is height or weight, as your height could be 150.1 cm – that's not a whole number! For example, let's say we are conducting an experiment to find out how much children grow between the ages of seven and ten. We could measure the height of an individual student between those ages – in this case, Alisha – and collect our results in a table like this:

AGE (years)	HEIGHT (cm)
7	122.5
8	127.8
9	129.1
10	132

We can present the data in a line graph like this:

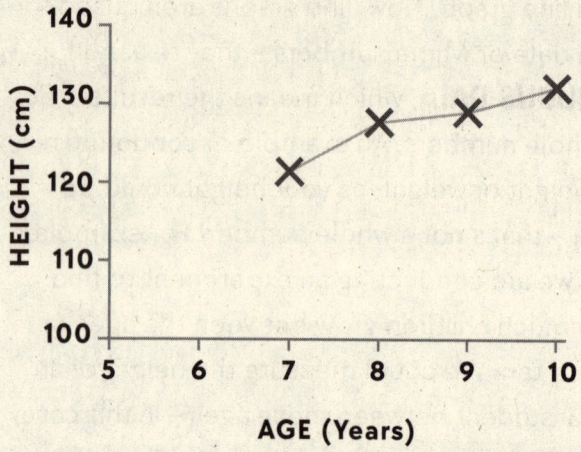

The numbers along the X axis (the row at the bottom) show Alisha's age, and the numbers along the Y axis (the column at the side) show her height. If you trace your finger along the line, you can see that as Alisha's age goes up, her height also goes up. On a line graph, we can't present the data in any order, as this would make the data harder to interpret. If we mixed up the order of the ages on the X axis, then the graph wouldn't really make sense, init. Line graphs are often used to show how data changes over time, so in this case we can see how height increases with age. **BOOM**, done know!

SCATTER GRAPHS

We're going to take a look at one more type of graph – this one's called a scatter graph. A scatter graph can show you the relationship between two sets of data, and they're a bit different to line graphs. On line graphs, we have the variable that we're measuring on the Y axis (Alisha's height), and the variable that changes on the X axis (her age). But on scatter graphs, we have a variable that is measured on both the X and Y axes.

For example, let's say that as part of our experiment, we measure the heights of four students. We could put this data on to a scatter graph and compare it to another set of data – for example, the amount of food in grams each student eats in a day. Now we're comparing the height of the four students with the amount of food they eat in a day. This will allow us to see the **correlation**, or the relationship, between height and how much food someone eats. **Correlation basically means the patterns between the variables.**

So for this scatter graph, we can see that the taller a student is, the more food they eat in a day. However, just because these two variables are correlated (or related), it doesn't mean that one causes the other. In other words, just because height increases as food intake increases, that doesn't mean the increase in height is caused by the increase in food. Your height is influenced by many different things, including your genes – the parts of your cells that are inherited from your parents and which control things like your eye colour and height.

STUDENT	HEIGHT (cm)	FOOD EATEN PER DAY (g)
Leeroy	122.5	1,000
Rachel	127.8	1,100
James	135	1,300
Alisha	132	1,350

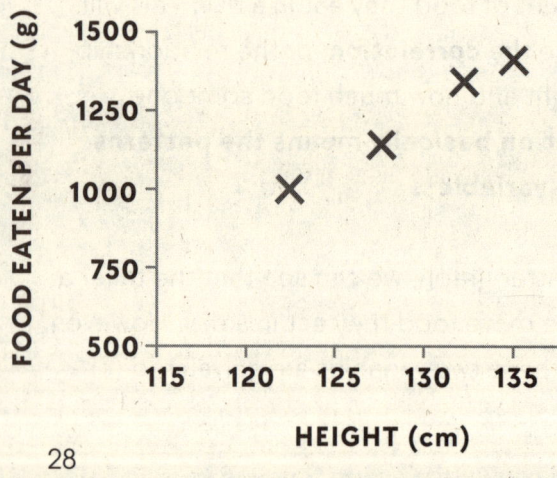

CHECK YOUR SOURCES!

OK BOOM! Now we know how to collect and present our data. Is there anything else we need to know to become proper scientists?

Yes, there is – it's really important as scientists that we check our sources. A source is something we can go to for information. There's bare different places we can gather information, like books, the internet and even people. There are two main types of sources: **PRiMARY** and **SECONDARY SOURCES**.

Let's start with primary sources. The information that you gather from your own investigations and experiments is called primary-source information. Whereas when you search for information in a book or on the internet, you're getting a secondary source of information. This is because somebody else carried out the research, not you. So primary sources of information come from you, and secondary sources come from someone else.

Scientists use both primary and secondary sources of information as evidence to prove their ideas. And sometimes they use these sources to disagree with each other's ideas!

CHAPTER 1

When looking at secondary sources of information, it's very important that you check who is saying it and why. Not everything that you read on the internet is true! If you're looking up some information, it's best to go to a reliable source – in other words, a source you can trust. If you were looking up some data about health, for example, finding an article written by a doctor would be much more reliable than just searching on social media. It's also important to check your information against other sources – this is called **cross-referencing**. Cross-referencing makes your information more reliable by checking if the information you've found has been discovered elsewhere too.

Cool. Now we know all about how to conduct our experiments properly, collect and present our data, and make sure our sources are 100 per cent certified. Now it's time to get into some physics tings and start experimenting!

Before we move on, here's a quick summary of the key points we learned in this chapter:

★ **An independent variable is the thing we change.**

★ **A dependent variable is the thing we measure.**

★ **A control is the thing that stays the same throughout our experiment.**

★ **Bar charts are used for discrete data (whole numbers).**

★ **Line graphs are used for continuous data (not whole numbers).**

★ **Scatter graphs are used to compare two different sets of data.**

★ **Primary sources come from your own independent research.**

★ **Secondary sources from someone else's research.**

★ **Cross-referencing to verify both primary and secondary sources is bare important!**

CHAPTER 2

FEEL THE FORCE

ITE, BOOM! If we're gonna talk about physics tings, first we need to know about forces. So, what is a force? **A force is simply a push or pull on an object.** So right here we have two objects – you, and this book. You are pulling the pages of the book when you turn them, and that pull is a force. Pushing open a door also requires force. Even walking involves force when you push your feet against the ground. Almost every action that we do in our day-to-day lives requires a force to make it happen.

Have you ever played tug of war? That's a really good example of forces in action. Let's say you and your friend have the exact same strength and you play a game of tug of war. Who's gonna win? Probably no one, to be honest, because you'd both be pulling the rope with the exact same force. One person is pulling the rope in one direction and the other person in the opposite direction, but both forces are equal so they cancel each other out. So, the rope stays in the same place and doesn't move.

OK cool – so let's say one of you did a bit of exercise and got some muscles. Who do you think would win now? Most likely the person with bigger muscles because they could pull the rope with more force.

CHAPTER 2

The forces on each side of the rope are now unequal, as there is a greater force on one side than the other. As a result, the rope is pulled towards the side with greater force.

YOU GET ME? YOU DONE KNOW, FAM.

Let's go back to the tug of war example again, but this time, in the right corner we have the super-strong Heracles and in the left corner we have . . . the Gingerbread Man. But anyway, who do you think would win? Obviously Hercules, init, because he's bare strong – he'd win before you even get a chance to blink. That's because he can pull with an extreme force that makes the rope move quickly. This shows that if we increase the force, we can move things even quicker.

I CAN'T LIE, THIS IS A BIT OF AN UNEVEN MATCH UP STILL.

OK, but what if Heracles wanted to be nice to the Gingerbread Man, and decided to pull softly – what would happen then? Well, the rope would move much slower. This shows that if we decrease the force, things move more slowly. If both players gave up and stopped pulling, the rope wouldn't move. So, if you remove the force, then the object won't move.

Did you know force can be measured? We measure force in **newtons** (N). So, for example, pushing open a door only requires about 15–20 newtons of force, which isn't a lot at all, and that's why it's quite easy. But pushing a car can require 1,000 newtons – that's a mad ting.

I can't lie, yeah, we're going to step up the science a likkle bit now. Listen up – when it comes to forces, there's two main types. We have **CONTACT FORCES** and **NON-CONTACT FORCES**.

YOU MAY THINK YOU'RE STRONG ENOUGH TO PUSH IT, BUT TRUST ME, DON'T FORCE IT!

Contact might sound like a mad word but it's a lot simpler than it looks. To contact something just means to touch it. So, what's the difference between these two types of forces? Well, for a contact force to happen, the two objects must be physically touching. When you open a door, you must physically touch it and push it open, so this is a contact force.

On the other hand, for a non-contact force to happen, the objects don't need to be physically touching. Like in a magnetic force, for example – the magnet pulls in metals without actually touching them. That's a non-contact (non-touching) force. We're gonna learn a bit more about magnets later on in this book.

FRICTION (NOT FICTION!)

First we're going to look at a contact force called **friction**. Now, I'm not talking about those books you read that have made-up stories in them – that's *fiction*, fam. We're talking about friction here.

Friction is a force between two surfaces that are sliding over each other, or are at least trying to! Like if you were to push a box along a carpet, friction would make it difficult so you'd have to push quite hard. Friction slows the box down, because it works in the opposite direction to the direction the box is moving in. So, you're pushing the box forward, but friction is pushing it backwards so it travels slower.

But what would happen if we switched the surface to a smooth, polished wooden floor? The box would move bare quick still. That's because there's less friction, init, so it would be easier as it's not being slowed down as much. But why is the friction different on different surfaces?

Well, it's because different surfaces have different **textures**. Texture is what a surface feels like when you touch it. Some surfaces are super silky smooth, so objects can slide over them easily. But other surfaces are really rough and bumpy, so it's more difficult for objects to slide over them. The smoother the surface, the less friction is produced, and the rougher the surface, the more friction is produced. Friction also produces a lot of heat – rub your hands together for about fifteen seconds and they'll get bare warm! The faster two objects are sliding over each other, the more friction there is. This means more heat will also be produced.

EXPERIMENT 1: FRICTION IN ACTION!

Ite cool, that's enough talking. I think it's time to do a friction experiment. We're going to pick up a bottle using a single chopstick. But if you don't have chopsticks, don't worry, a pencil works just as well.

AIM: To create friction!

HYPOTHESIS:

_____

_____

_____

> NO – iT'S NOT DiNNER TiME, FAM, iT'S EXPERiMENT TiME!

Equipment:
★ a pencil/chopstick
★ a small plastic water or soda bottle
★ uncooked rice (enough to almost fill the bottle)

METHOD

1. Pour the uncooked rice into the bottle until it's nearly full, leaving a small gap at the top.

2. Use the chopstick/pencil to push the rice down into the bottle. Tap and shake the bottle to help the rice fill in the gaps. The tighter it's packed, the more friction there will be.

3. Push the pencil into the middle of the rice in the bottle.

4. Once the pencil is firmly in the rice, gently lift the pencil upwards.

RESULTS

When the pencil was lifted, the bottle came with it!

CONCLUSION

Why does the bottle lift up? Well, it's cos the rice grains are tightly packed round the pencil, so there is friction between the pencil and the rice grains. The force of the friction is stronger than the force used to pull the pencil out of the rice, so the pencil stays in the rice. The friction between the rice and pencil is strong enough to lift the entire bottle!

EVALUATION

How did your experiment go, fam? Did it work as you expected? Write down any observations here:

_____

_____

_____

_____

_____

_____

ICE SKATING ON RUBBER!

Have you ever been ice skating before? You know when you're getting ready to go do some mad skating – then your skates are on and you stand up on that rubbery floor. But what would happen if you tried to skate on that rubber floor? Well firstly, please don't try that, because you'll DEFO end up falling over! And secondly, there's no way you would be able to do it because there's just too much friction between your skates and the rubber. Yet as soon as you step out on to the ice, your skates glide over it effortlessly. That's because there's very likkle friction between your skates and the ice. This tells us that **different surfaces have different levels of friction**. We're actually going to prove this now with a quick experiment . . .

EXPERIMENT 2: SURFACE LEVEL

So, this experiment is bare simple, yeah. We're going to push a toy car or ball on grass, carpet, concrete and smooth flooring and see which surface has the most friction. The car or ball will travel furthest on the surface with the least friction, and it'll travel the shortest distance on the surface with the most friction. Which surface do you think will have the most friction?

AIM: Investigate how much friction different surfaces have.

HYPOTHESIS: I think the _____ will have the most friction, followed by the _____, _____ and then _____.

Equipment:
★ a toy car or small ball
★ different surfaces (wooden or laminate floor, carpet, grass, concrete)
★ a tape measure or ruler

METHOD

1. Push the toy car on the wooden or laminate floor and measure the distance travelled with the tape measure, making sure to push with the same force each time.

2. Repeat for carpet, grass and concrete.

RESULTS

Fill in your results in the table below! What type of graph would be most suitable for the results of your experiment?

SURFACE TYPE	DISTANCE TRAVELLED BY TOY CAR (cm)
Wooden floor	
Carpet	
Grass	
Concrete	

CONCLUSION

My hypothesis was **CORRECT / INCORRECT**.

The car travelled _____cm on the grass, which is the
LONGEST / SHORTEST distance.

This means the grass has the **MOST / LEAST** friction,
followed by the **CONCRETE / WOODEN FLOOR /
CARPET**.

The wooden floor had the **MOST / LEAST** friction,
as the car travelled _____cm, which is the
FURTHEST / SHORTEST distance.

EVALUATION

How did this experiment go? Did you manage to keep
all your controls the same, like making sure you used the
same force each time? What else might have affected
your results? If it was raining outside, that could have
also changed the results because the rain would've made
surfaces more slippery!

MORE FRICTION IN ACTION . . .

Let me give you an example of friction in real life. We've all been there before – sitting in the bath for too long and your fingers turn into wrinkly likkle raisins. Well, those likkle wrinkles make the surface of our fingertips rougher, which increases the friction. This makes it easier for us to hold and grip things, because there's more friction between our fingers and the object, so it's less likely to fall out of our hand. And we need more friction when we're in a wet place, such as a bath, because water makes things slippy!

BE RIGHT BACK. IT'S BATH TIME NOW!

Another example is when we're walking on the pavement with shoes on. There's friction between the tread of our shoes and the pavement, and this grips the ground to stop our feet from sliding. So, friction can be useful sometimes. And if you've ever walked on ice before then you know how slippery it is – there's hardly any friction between the bottom of our shoes and the ice, so we can't grip the ground properly.

Friction can be a bit of a pain sometimes though, especially when it happens between two metals sliding over each other. If you've ever heard a door creak, then you'll know what I'm talking about. That sound is caused by metal pieces in the door's hinge sliding over each when the door is opened or closed. To stop it from creaking, we need to reduce the friction between the metals. This is done by spraying them with an oil. The oil flows in between the two metals and creates a thin barrier, meaning that they're no longer touching each other and so can't make that creaking sound. We can say that the oil lubricates the metals.

DONE KNOW!

ITE, BOOM! Man's got five different surfaces here, and we're gonna see which ones are rough and which are smooth. Our surfaces are concrete, wooden floor, carpet, grass, sand and a tile floor. Complete the table by saying whether these surfaces are rough or smooth. I'll start you off . . .

SURFACE TYPE	TEXTURE
Concrete	Rough
Wooden floor	
Carpet	
Grass	
Sand	
Tile floor	

FRICTION AND AIR

So, we know that friction can happen between two solid objects when they slide over each other, but it can also happen between a solid object and a gas, such as air. This type of friction is called **air resistance**, and it happens when an object is moving through a gas.

Just like friction in solids, air resistance also acts in the direction opposite to the direction that the object is moving in. The faster an object is travelling through air, the more air resistance there will be. A falling feather is a perfect example of air resistance. As it falls, there's friction between the feather and air particles. The weight of the feather makes it fall downwards, but air resistance pushes it upwards. This slows down the feather as it falls. That's why it slowly floats to the ground!

The shape of an object also has a big effect on how much air resistance it has when travelling through air. Thin, long and pointy objects have less air resistance than short and wide objects with a large

surface area. (Surface area just means how much space the surface of an object takes up.) That's why aeroplanes have a long body and a pointy nose. This allows the plane to fly forward without the air pushing it backwards too much and slowing it down. Aeroplanes have a streamlined design – this means they create the least possible air resistance.

PLANES ARE BARE FAST, FAM!

EXPERIMENT 3:
AIR RESISTANCE IN ACTION

We can actually show air resistance right now – all we need is a pen and paper. Now this experiment is bare simple . . .

AIM: To investigate the effects of air resistance by dropping two objects.

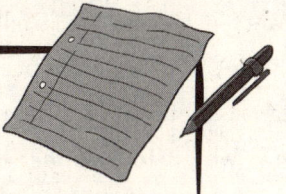

Equipment:
★ a pen
★ a piece of paper

HYPOTHESIS: I think the _____
will hit the ground first.

METHOD

1. Pick up the pen and paper in each hand.

2. Hold them above your head.

3. Drop them on to the floor and observe which hits the floor first.

RESULTS

The paper took longer to hit the ground than the pen.

CONCLUSION

The pen hit the ground first because it has a long, thin and pointy shape. This reduced the amount of air resistance it created, so it fell faster. The paper has a wide shape and large surface area, so it created more air resistance as it fell. This air resistance slowed it down, which is why it took longer to fall.

DID YOU KNOW THAT FRICTION CAN ALSO HAPPEN IN WATER TOO? WHEN WE SWIM, THE FRICTION BETWEEN OUR SKIN AND THE WATER SLOWS US DOWN. THIS IS KNOWN AS WATER RESISTANCE!

EVALUATION

This is a pretty simple experiment, fam, but is there anything you could do differently? Maybe you could time how long it took for both objects to hit the ground using a stopwatch, which would make your experiment more accurate.

EXPERIMENT 4: PAPER AEROPLANES

ITE, BOOM! We're gonna try another air resistance experiment now.

Let's make two paper aeroplanes with different shapes to see how this affects how they fly through the air. The first one is going to be a standard paper aeroplane, but the second one is going to be a dart.

AIM: To investigate how the shape of an aeroplane affects air resistance.

HYPOTHESIS: I think the _____ plane will have less air resistance.

Equipment:
★ Two pieces of A4 paper

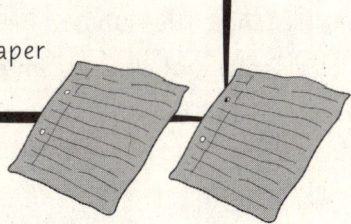

METHOD

1. Fold the A4 paper into a standard aeroplane. (go to p.194 for some instructions!)

2. Fold the other paper into a dart aeroplane (go to p.196 for this one fam).

3. Fly them one at a time and observe which one is faster.

RESULTS

The dart airplane was faster than the standard aeroplane.

CONCLUSION

The dart aeroplane is more streamlined, so it had less air resistance. The standard aeroplane has a wider shape with a larger surface area, which meant it had more air resistance and travelled slower.

EVALUATION

How did this experiment go? Perhaps you could try some other paper aeroplane shapes by looking some up online, then compare how the different shapes perform!

If an object has a bigger surface area, there will be more air resistance, so it will fall slower. Let's take skydivers, for example — when they're falling, they use parachutes with big surface areas to slow themselves down using air resistance. The larger the surface area of an object, the more air resistance it will have when falling. This is because it catches more air, which slows down its fall.

TALKING OF PARACHUTES, SHALL WE MAKE ONE RIGHT NOW? LET'S DO IT, MAN!

EXPERIMENT 5: MAKING A PARACHUTE

> ## Ask a grown-up to help you with this one!

What we're going to do is get a small weight like a toy or Lego figure (or a small stone). Then we're gonna build our toy or stone a likkle parachute before dropping it from a height. Before we begin though, let's make our hypothesis. What do we think will happen? Let's find out.

AIM: To find out how a parachute affects a falling object.

HYPOTHESIS: I think the parachute will decrease the weight's speed.

Equipment:
*   ★ a plastic bag
*   ★ some thread/string
*   ★ some tape
*   ★ a small weight (toy, Lego, stone)
*   ★ a pair of scissors

METHOD

1. Cut the plastic bag into a square or circle about 35 cm x 35 cm (get an adult to help you!).

2. Cut four equal lengths of string to around 30 cm long each.

3. Tape or tie the ends of the string to the four corners or edges of the parachute material. If using a circular parachute, space out strings evenly.

4. Tie or tape the other ends of the four strings to your chosen weight. Make sure the strings are centred so the weight hangs evenly.

5. Go to a high place, such as standing on a chair or up a few stairs, and drop the parachute into a clear space. Observe what happens as it floats down.

6. Remove the parachute from the weight and drop it from the same height. Observe how it falls.

RESULTS

With the parachute, the weight fell to the ground slower compared to without the parachute.

CONCLUSION

My hypothesis was correct: the parachute caused the weight to fall to the ground more slowly. The air resistance from the falling parachute slowed down the speed of the weight, so it floated gently to the ground.

EVALUATION

Did you make sure to keep your controls the same?

LET'S GET MECHANICAL

OK, now we've learned a bit about forces, I'm gonna introduce you to another area of physics called mechanics. This is basically the area of physics that deals with forces and how they act on objects. Mechanics literally make our world work – they're behind every machine you've ever used, from big machines like elevators to small ones like scissors.

The most basic machines are known as **SIMPLE MACHINES**. Simple machines can help us to move objects by changing the direction of a force or reducing the amount of force that's needed.

One example of a simple machine is a **PULLEY**. Pulleys are useful because they help us to lift heavy objects. Imagine you're struggling trying to carry a heavy box, then someone pops up and carries it from the opposite side – it's gonna feel bare light now. Well, pulleys work in the same way. They lift some of the weight of the object, which means we don't have to work as hard.

CHAPTER 2

So what does a pulley look like? A pulley is a wheel on a **fixed axle**. Wait, hold up – we know what a wheel is, but what's a fixed axle? That simply means that's it's a wheel that spins, but the axle – the bit in the middle of the wheel that it is attached to – doesn't move. So basically, like when you lift a bike's wheel up in the air and spin it the wheel spins round the axle, but the bike's not moving anywhere.

You see window blinds, yeah? They use pulleys! Blinds have a rope hanging from the top that you pull to make them go up. The rope runs along a wheel on a fixed axle. This wheel has a groove in it that helps to guide the rope through. On one end of the rope, we have the weight to be lifted, which is the blind. At the other end of the rope, we have the person who is lifting. When you pull the rope, some of the weight is lifted by the pulley, so it's easier for you to lift. The weight is shared between the pulley and your hands.

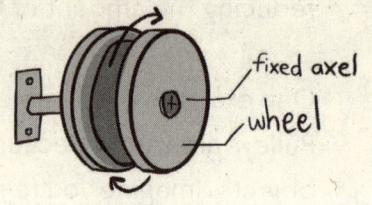

fixed axel

wheel

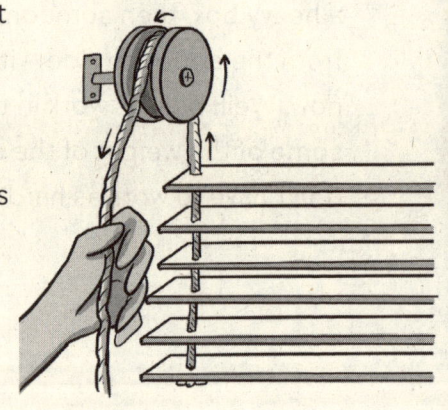

The more pulleys you use, the easier it is to lift something. Elevators use pulleys too, but instead of ropes, they have big, thick cables. Some of these cables are strong enough to lift thousands of kilograms – that's bare people! Pulleys are also used by cranes – that's why they can lift heavy construction equipment like steel and bricks.

You might have seen a flag being raised on a flagpole by a rope. That's also a pulley system!

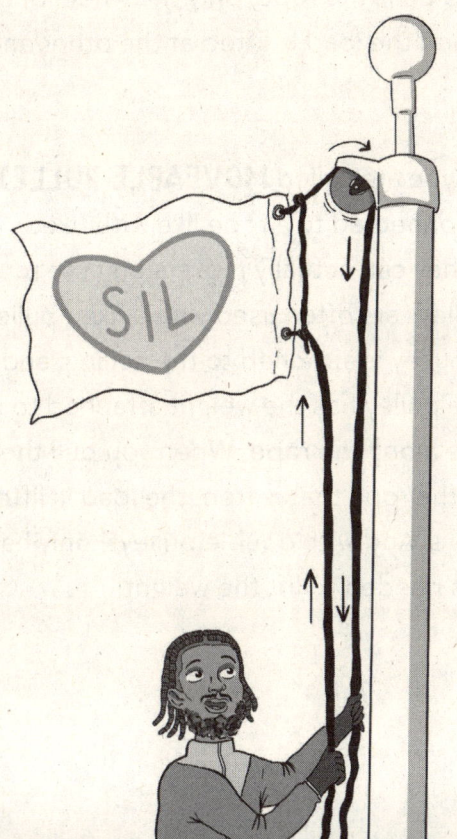

When it comes to pulleys, there are two main types. The first are **FIXED PULLEYS**. Why are they called fixed pulleys?

> YEAH, YOU'VE GUESSED iT – BECAUSE THEY'RE FiXED!

So, in other words, they don't move. Blinds use fixed pulleys. Fixed pulleys are usually attached to something like a ceiling or roof. When someone on the ground pulls the rope, only the wheel of the pulley spins and the load is lifted at the other end of the rope.

The second type are called **MOVEABLE PULLEYS**. They're still connected to a rope like with fixed pulleys, but they can actually move along the rope. Moveable pulleys are often used with a fixed pulley – so the fixed pulley is attached to the ceiling, and the moveable pulley has the weight attached to it and can move along the rope. When you pull the other end of the rope that is free, the load is lifted by both pulleys. And with double pulleys, only half as much force is needed to lift the weight!

FIXED PULLEY

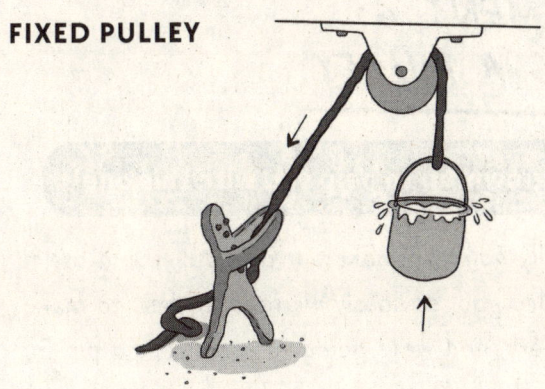

MOVEABLE PULLEY

I'M GOING TO *PULL* YOU AWAY FOR A MOMENT SO WE CAN EXPERIMENT WITH PULLEYS. LET'S GO!

EXPERIMENT 6: MAKING A PULLEY

Ask a grown-up to help you with this one!

We're actually going to make our own pulley and use it to lift an object. So, obviously we need a wheel to make our pulley work, and we're going to use a rolling pin for this. Do you think it'll be easier to lift an object up with or without the pulley? Write down your hypothesis!

AIM: To find out if a pulley makes it easier to lift an object.

HYPOTHESIS: I think I will be able to lift an object using less effort with the pulley.

Equipment:
★ a sturdy surface to attach the pulley to (table/chairs)
★ a rolling pin
★ some string or a rope
★ a bucket/container with a handle
★ different weights (bag of rice, bag of sugar, rock)

METHOD

1. Create a support for the pulley using two chairs. Rest the ends of the rolling pin on each chair so that it can roll freely.

2. Cut a piece of string long enough to reach from the ground to over the rolling pin, and back to the ground on the other side.

3. Tie one end of the string to the handle of the bucket/container.

4. Place one of the weights into the bucket.

5. Ensure that the string is sitting on the rolling pin.

6. Ask someone to hold down the ends of the rolling pin. Pull the string and test how easy it is to lift it compared to without the pulley.

RESULTS

The objects were much easier to lift using the pulley compared to without it.

CONCLUSION

My hypothesis was correct. The objects were easier to lift when the pulley was used. This is because the pulley carried some of the weight of the object, which meant I could lift it with less effort.

EVALUATION

How did this experiment go? Is there anything you would do differently next time?

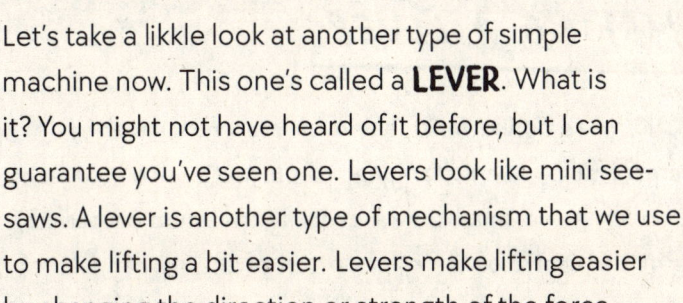

WHAT ARE LEVERS?

Let's take a likkle look at another type of simple machine now. This one's called a **LEVER**. What is it? You might not have heard of it before, but I can guarantee you've seen one. Levers look like mini see-saws. A lever is another type of mechanism that we use to make lifting a bit easier. Levers make lifting easier by changing the direction or strength of the force.

Levers have three main parts: the **load**, the **fulcrum** and the **effort**:

★ The load is simply the thing that's being lifted.

★ The fulcrum – also known as the pivot – is the spot the lever sits on. Usually, you have a long piece of material called a bar, which balances on top of the fulcrum too, and the lever moves up and down or around it.

★ The effort is the power that we use to lift the load (either with a machine or our muscles).

Now, if you're finding this a bit tricky to understand then don't worry, we're going to make our own lever so we can see the different parts in action . . .

EXPERIMENT 7: MAKING A LEVER

OK, we're gonna make our own lever. First, grab an eraser (it can be rectangular or one with curved edges), a ruler and a small toy (a Lego figure would be perfect). Put the centre of the ruler on top of the rubber. Put the Lego toy at one end of the ruler. You've literally just made a lever!

AIM: To build a lever.

HYPOTHESIS: I think one end of the lever will pop up when we press down on the other end.

Equipment:
★ an eraser
★ a ruler
★ a small toy

METHOD

1. Balance the ruler on top of the eraser so both ends of the ruler are off the surface.

2. Place the toy at one end of the ruler.

3. Push down on the opposite end of the ruler to make the lever pop up!

RESULTS

When we pressed down on one end of the lever, the other end lifted up the toy.

CONCLUSION

In this example, the ruler is the bar, the eraser is the pivot or fulcrum, and the toy is the load. When the free end of the ruler is pushed down (the effort), the load (toy) is lifted up!

EVALUATION

I'm not gonna lie, this experiment is bare simple so there's not a lot to evaluate here . . . !

CHAPTER 2

I'M GONNA LEVEL WITH YOU . . .

Remember how in our experiment we pushed down on the lever, but the toy lifted up? This is because some of the weight was lifted by the fulcrum (pivot).

OK, now instead of having the fulcrum in the middle of the bar, what would happen if we moved it to the end? Then the load would be in the middle of the bar, the effort would be at the other end. We've just described a wheelbarrow! The wheel of the wheelbarrow is the fulcrum, and the two handles at the end where you lift it are the effort. Right in the middle, we have a load such as rocks or bricks. Wheelbarrows use a lever mechanism to decrease the amount of effort needed to lift a load. Can you imagine trying to lift all those bricks by hand? That would take bare long.

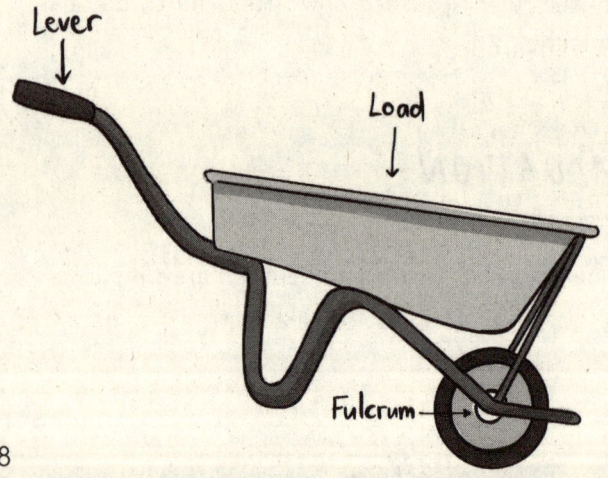

Lever

Load

Fulcrum

But what if we leave the fulcrum at one end, and instead of having the load in the middle, we put it at the other end this time. We then put the effort in the middle. Now we've got a shovel! Shovels have the load at one end – the soil being lifted. In the middle, yeah, that's where we hold it and put our effort. The end closest to you is the fulcrum.

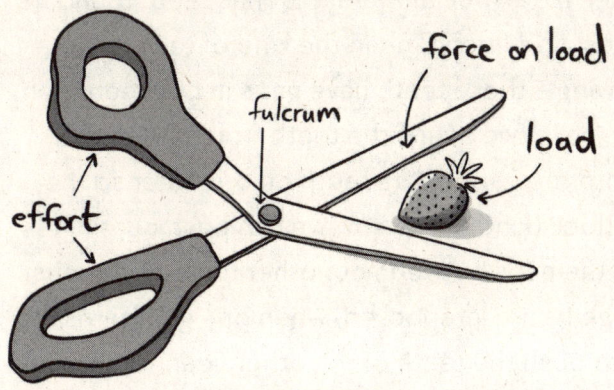

Another example of levers in everyday life is a pair of scissors. You see the screw that connects the two scissor blades together? That's the fulcrum. When two levers are connected, it's called a **linkage**. In a linkage, levers work together and can move with different amounts of force and in different directions (depending on the type of linkage). Folding chairs, the arm of a digger, and a pair of garden shears all use linkages!

LEVEL UP

CHAPTER 2

WHAT ARE GEARS?

Ite cool, now we're going to kick it up a gear! A **GEAR** is another type of mechanism, but this one isn't a simple machine – it's what we call a **COMPLEX MACHINE**. Let's get into it . . .

So, a gear is basically a wheel – but not just any wheel; it's a special wheel that has teeth round its edges. And I don't mean the kind of teeth we use for chewing – these teeth have gaps in between them. If we have two gears, the teeth from one gear can fit into the gaps of the teeth on the other so they interlock (kind of like how we can push our fingers into the gaps between our other fingers). Because the gears are interlocked, when one gear turns, its teeth push the teeth of the other gear, which causes the other gear to turn too. So one gear transfers movement and motion to another, which helps something to move. Gears are used in machines like bikes, cars and clocks to help them change speed and direction.

I hope you're feeling geared up, because we're going to go into a likkle bit more detail . . .

So gears come in different sizes, init – some are big and some are small. Big gears turn a lot slower than the small ones because, well, they're big, you get me? To explain why, I want you to imagine you're in a playground. In this playground we have two circles of different sizes, which represent a big gear and a small gear. The big circle is a massive racetrack that surrounds the whole playground, but the small circle is a hula hoop that we've put on the ground. Which circle is going to take the longest to run around? Well, obviously the racetrack! You have a longer distance to travel on the racetrack, so it will take a longer time to complete it.

RACETRACK SETTINGS!

CHAPTER 2

It's the same thing with the larger gear. Its big size means that it just takes longer for it make one full turn. The smaller gear only has a small distance to move to make a full turn, so it turns much quicker. So, what does this mean if we have a big gear turning a small gear? When we rotate the big gear, it will turn slowly, but it will make the smaller gear rotate much faster. This means if a big gear turns a smaller gear, we can increase the speed.

But changing gear size doesn't only change the speed – it also changes how much force and power the gear has. A large gear may turn more slowly, but it has waaay more teeth than a smaller one. The greater number of teeth allows it to grip more on the next gear, so it can transfer more force. So if the second wheel in a pair of gears is larger than the first one, it will turn slower than the first gear but with more power. So changing the size of a gear makes a big difference to the power, speed and direction of a machine such as a bike or car.

A perfect example of this is riding a bike. Bikes have two main gears – the front gear near the pedal, and the back gear on the back wheel. These two gears are linked by the bikes chain. When you pedal, the front gear turns. This motion is transferred to the smaller back gear, and it turns more quickly. This fast turning of the back gear then turns the wheel of the bike, and it moves.

Some bikes – like mountain bikes for example – have more than one back gear. These gears are differently sized, and you can switch between gears. If you choose a larger gear, you will travel more slowly because larger gears take longer to make one full turn. This means it will also take longer for the wheel of the bike to turn. But remember, **larger gears produce more power because they have more teeth and more grip**, which makes it easier to cycle.

That's why we use larger back gears when pedalling uphill, as the extra teeth give us extra force to make the bike move, meaning we don't have to pedal as hard.

But if you choose a smaller gear, you can travel faster. This is because smaller gears turn more quickly, so the wheel of the bike will also turn faster. However, smaller gears have fewer teeth, so there's less grip between gears, which makes it harder to pedal. That's why we don't use small gears for uphill cycling!

ITE, BOOM! We've kicked things off and learned about some big physics tings, from friction to mechanics. Nice one, fam! Next, we're gonna learn about another big area of physics: sound. But before you turn over to the next chapter, let's have a quick reminder of what we learned about forces:

★ A contact force happens between two objects that are physically touching.

★ A non-contact force happens between two objects that aren't physically touching.

★ Force is measured in newtons (N).

★ Friction slows down the speed of an object.

★ Rough surfaces produce more friction than smooth surfaces.

★ Friction produces heat.

★ Air resistance is friction between a moving object and air.

★ The larger the surface area of an object, the greater the air resistance.

★ Simple machines can help us to lift, move or pull objects because they change the direction of a force or the amount of force that's required.

★ Levers and pulleys are examples of simple machines, and can help us to lift things up using less force.

★ Gears allow machines to change speed, direction and power.

★ Bigger gears produce more power than smaller gears.

★ Smaller gears produce more speed than bigger gears.

CHAPTER 3

SOUNDS
GOOD

ITE COOL, SO WHAT IS SOUND?

Sound is simply anything that you can hear with our ears.

Like your voice, for example – that's sound.

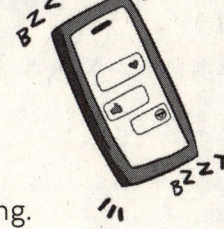

Or your favourite song.

Even the rustling of the pages in this book as you turn them.

These are all sounds. But where do they come from? Well, sound is energy that comes from an object vibrating. And what does 'vibrating' mean? It's really just a fancy way of saying 'moving quickly forward and backwards'.

SUPER SOUND

CHARACTERISTICS
Great vibes

Can be a bit loud
sometimes – sound
can be loud or quiet.

LOVES ♥
Chilling with a guitar
or piano – musical
instruments create
sound!

GOOD AT
Setting the mood –
some sounds can make
us feel happy or relaxed.

Let's look at a real-life example of vibrations. If you hold a basketball in your hand and drop it on the floor, the ball will begin to vibrate. See how the ball looks like it's shaking as it bounces? That's it vibrating.

ITE, BOOM! **So, we know sound is caused by vibrations, but how does it travel?** Does it just grab a suitcase and hop on a plane? Well, obviously not – that would be a mad ting still!

Let's go back to our basketball example. The vibrations from the ball cause the air around it to vibrate as well. When an air molecule moves, it bumps into the molecule next to it, causing it to move too. The vibration is passed on through the air molecules like a chain reaction. It's kind of like when you push one domino and it knocks down the next one, creating a domino effect. This movement of energy is called a **sound-wave**.

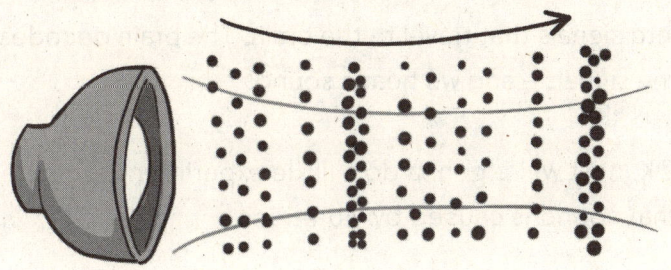

CHAPTER 3

Now, this wave isn't like a wave in the ocean. The movement of a sound-wave is a bit more like how a slinky moves, where each metal coil pushes on the one in front to move the slinky forward. The air molecules vibrate back and forth in the same direction that the sound is moving, each knocking into the one in front.

When the vibrating air enters our ear, it hits our **ear drum**. The ear drum is a thin membrane inside your ear that vibrates when a sound-wave hits it. As the ear drum vibrates,

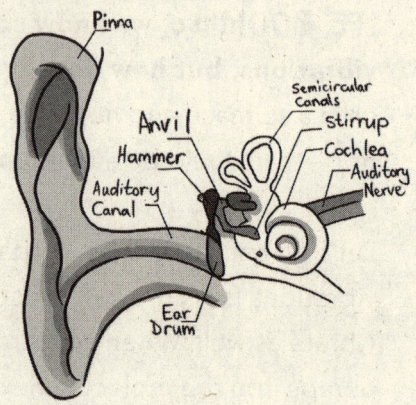

it sets off another chain reaction inside your ear. The three small bones attached to the ear drum – called the **ossicles** – start vibrating too. The vibrations finally enter your inner ear (or **cochlea**), which is shaped like a snail shell and full of tiny hairs. The tiny hairs pick up the movements of the sound-waves and turn these into signals that travel to the brain. The brain decodes the signals – and we hear a sound!

OK, next we're gonna do a likkle experiment to prove that sound is caused by vibrations.

EXPERIMENT 8: GOOD VIBRATIONS

So, this experiment is actually bare simple, yeah — we're gonna stretch a rubber band over a plastic tub and pluck it like we're playing a guitar. You done know, music ting. First, we're just going to pluck it normally and see what happens. Then, we're going to pinch the rubber band with our fingers quickly after we pluck it. What do you think will happen?

AIM: To find out if vibration produces sound.

HYPOTHESIS: I think that the rubber band will make a sound/vibrate with the first pluck. After the second pluck, the rubber band will stop vibrating when we pinch it, and the sound will also stop.

Equipment:
★ a rubber band
★ a plastic tub

METHOD

1. Stretch the rubber band over the tub — this is our 'guitar'.

2. Pluck the rubber band once and observe what happens.

3. Pluck the rubber band a second time, but this time, pinch it quickly after plucking.

4. Write down your observations.

RESULTS

The rubber band made a sound and vibrated with the first pluck. On the second pluck — when we pinched the rubber band — it stopped vibrating, and the sound also stopped.

CONCLUSION

From our experiment, we can conclude that plucking a rubber band causes it to vibrate. This vibration produces sound. When we pinched the rubber band, the vibration stopped along with the sound. So, our hypothesis was correct!

EVALUATION

Is there anything we could have done differently? Maybe you could try recording the different sounds on a phone?

SOUND IN AIR

BOOM! So, we've learned that sound is caused by vibrations that travel through the air. Our experiment showed us that when the vibrations stop, the sound stops too. Let's try another example real quick. Clap your hands together and listen. The sound travelled through the air from your hands to your ears. Now, I want you to read this sentence aloud. Read it again, but this time, cup your hand over your mouth. Did you hear a difference? Your voice became quieter with your mouth covered. This is because the air was blocked from exiting your mouth, and sound needs air to be heard. If we removed all the air, we wouldn't be able to hear anything because the sound wouldn't have anything to travel through via the molecules. A space with no air is called a **vacuum** (and I don't mean the one you use to hoover up dust). I mean like in outer space, where there's no air, and astronauts need to use oxygen tanks to breathe – that's a vacuum.

YOU DONE KNOW!

Sound-waves travel incredibly fast, even faster than a plane. The speed of sound in air is 760 miles per hour (mph). That's a mad ting!

SOUND IN SOLIDS AND LIQUIDS

But it's not just air that sound can travel through. There are three different states of matter: solids, liquids and gases, and sound can travel through all three of them. The substance that the sound is travelling through is called the **medium**, and it travels at different speeds depending on the medium it's in. Sound actually travels faster through liquids than air – the speed of sound in water is 3,218 miles per hour. That's over four times faster than the speed of sound through air!

However, sound travels fastest through solids. Sound can reach speeds of over 11,000 mph through solids (depending on the solid). That's crazy! I can actually show you how fast sound travels through solids. It's really simple – go to a table, preferably a wooden one. Now knock on it and see what you hear. Ite cool, now knock on it again – but this time, put your ear right up close to the table. What did you notice? It sounded bare loud, init! Why?

Sound travels best through solids because the particles in a solid are packed together really tightly. As the particles are so close together, the vibrations can travel quickly between them, whereas in a gas –

such as air – the particles are spread farther apart, so it takes longer for an air particle to bump into the next one to pass on the vibration. This slows the sound-wave down. In liquids, the particles are a bit closer together, so sound can travel faster in water than air. But solid particles are packed together the tightest, which is why sound travels fastest through them.

CHAPTER 3

ECHO, ECHO ECHO . . . !

Just like light, sound-waves can also be reflected off objects and surfaces. When a sound-wave is reflected, it's called an **echo**. Imagine standing at the edge of the Grand Canyon and shouting at the top of your lungs! The sound would travel into the canyon and be reflected back to you as an echo. So, you'd hear the exact same sound you made just a few seconds after you heard it, because the sound-waves are reflected off the rocks and came back to you.

ECHO TING!

ECHO TING!

ECHO TING!

You know that's how dolphins know where they're going underwater, right? They use echoes as part of a really cool process called echolocation. This is when dolphins make sounds that bounce off rocks and fish in the sea, and which are then reflected back to the dolphin. The further away an object is from the dolphin, the longer it takes for the reflected sound to reach them. The closer an object is to the dolphin, the quicker the reflected sound reaches them. So, the dolphin can work out how far away things are by how long it takes the sound to reflect back at them. That is absolutely crazy, fam!

WHAT IS PITCH?

OK cool, so we know what sound is and how it travels, but what is **pitch**? I'm not talking about a green field that you kick a football on. I mean the pitch of a sound. To explain it, I'm going to ask you a question:

Why do adults' voices sound different to children's voices?

One of the reasons is pitch. Children usually have higher-pitched voices, whereas adults have lower-pitched ones. The pitch of a sound is just how high or low it is. Simple tings. Pitch can be high like a squeaking mouse, or low like rumbling thunder.

We're going to dig a likkle bit deeper here. Remember the scientific name for the movement of sound energy? Sound-waves. Well, sound-waves can either be long or short. If it's a long sound-wave, then it's a low-pitched sound. If it's a short sound-wave, then it's a high-pitched sound. Easy. High-pitched sounds cause the air to vibrate quickly, whereas low-pitched sounds cause slower vibrations. We call the distance between each sound-wave the **wavelength**. Have a look at the diagrams below and opposite to compare shorter and longer wavelengths:

LOW PITCH

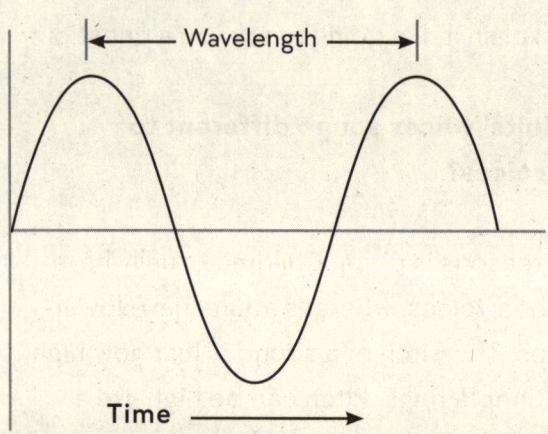

WE OFTEN DRAW SOUND-WAVES LIKE THIS – GOING UP AND DOWN – BUT REMEMBER, THE WAVE IS ACTUALLY MORE LIKE A SLINKY PUSHING FORWARD AND BACK.

HIGH PITCH

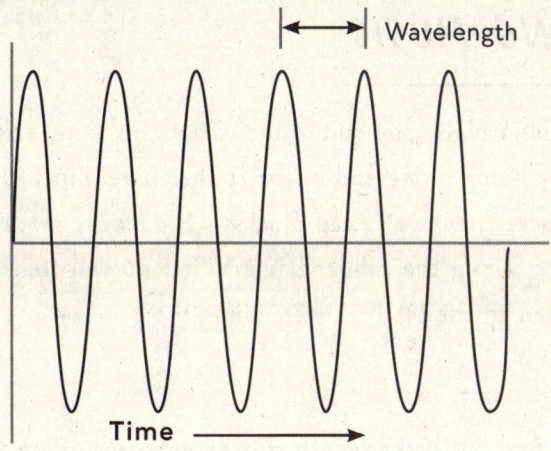

Wavelength

Time →

We can actually do an experiment to show how long and short sound-waves sound different.

ITE, BOOM! GRAB THE GUITAR YOU MADE EARLIER, COS WE'RE GONNA PLAY SOME REAL MUSIC!

EXPERIMENT 9:
MAKING MUSIC

We're gonna pluck our guitar again, but this time, we're gonna try holding one end of the rubber band pinched as we pluck. Then, we'll keep plucking and slowly move our fingers along the rubber band. What do you think will happen to the pitch as we change the position of our fingers?

AIM: To find out if the length of a sound-wave affects the pitch of the sound.

HYPOTHESIS: I think that the rubber band will make a different pitch depending on where we pinch it.

Equipment:
★ a rubber band
★ a plastic tub

METHOD

1. Stretch the rubber band over the tub.

2. Pinch one end of the rubber band, then pluck the other.

3. Slowly move your fingers along the rubber band as you pluck.

4. Observe what happens and record your results.

RESULTS

The pitch of the sound made by the rubber band changed depending on where it was pinched. The longer the rubber band, the lower the pitch. The shorter the rubber band, the higher the pitch.

CONCLUSION

We can conclude that changing the length of the vibrating part of the rubber band changes the pitch of the sound. When you pluck the rubber band normally without pinching, the full length of the band vibrates. This means the sound-wave is long, so it makes a lower-pitched sound. But when you pinch the rubber band, the part that is vibrating is shortened. This means that the sound-wave is also shortened. And as we know, shorter sound-waves make higher-pitched sounds!

EVALUATION

What do you think went well about this experiment? Is there anything you could have done differently? Have a think, then write down your answer.

_____

_____

_____

_____

_____

_____

EXPERIMENT 10: DANCING SUGAR

OK cool. Now that we've got some music going, it's time to dance. This next one is called the dancing sugar experiment, so I hope you've brought your dancing shoes! Remember at the start of this book when I said that we can't see sound? Well, we're going to get a likkle glimpse of it right now! So, what we're going to do is create some sound-waves and direct them towards the sugar. What do you think will happen? Will the sugar dance?

AIM: To see what sound-waves look like!

HYPOTHESIS: I think the sound-waves will cause the sugar to dance.

Equipment:
★ some cling film   ★ a bowl
★ some sugar (though you could also use salt too if you don't have sugar)
★ a phone (ask your grown-up if you can borrow theirs!)

METHOD

1. Place a layer of cling film on top of the bowl to cover it.

2. Sprinkle some sugar on top of the cling film.

3. Shout or hum next to the bowl and observe what happens to the sugar.

4. Use the phone to play some music next to the sugar and observe what happens then.

5. Try different types of music, e.g. bass-heavy music.

RESULTS

The sound-waves caused the sugar granules to jump around.

CONCLUSION

Sound-waves are the movement of air. As sugar granules are very light, the movement of the air had enough force to cause them to be lifted up.

EVALUATION

What did you notice in this experiment? Which sound made the sugar jump the most? Is there anything you could try and do differently?

MEASURING PITCH

You know the pitch of a sound can be measured, right? Before I tell you how, I'm going to introduce you to a proper scientific word – **hertz**. Hertz (Hz) is the unit of measurement for pitch.

A high-pitched sound, like a chirping bird, for example, is 4,000 hertz, but a deep, roaring lion is only 50 hertz. The greater the number of hertz, the higher the pitch. The smaller the number of hertz, the lower the pitch.

Humans can only hear sounds that have a pitch of between 20 hertz and 20,000 hertz. We call this the frequency range for human hearing. If the pitch of a sound gets too high and goes above 20,000 hertz, then you wouldn't be able to hear it any more. And if the pitch goes below 20 hertz, then you wouldn't be able to hear it either.

But some animals can hear sounds that have a frequency above 20,000 hertz – dogs can hear between 45,000–67,000 hertz, and cats up to 60,000 hertz! That's a mad ting. But the animal with the maddest hearing ability is the greater wax moth. It can hear sounds of up to 300,000 hertz – that's insane!

It can probably hear you reading this sentence right now . . .

TURN UP THE VOLUME!

OK, so now we're gonna turn it up. **What is volume? It's simply how loud or quiet a sound is.** A loud sound has a high volume, whereas a quiet one has a low volume. Bigger vibrations produce louder sounds.

For example, if you talk loudly, your vocal cords –
the small muscles in your throat that move to let air
through and make sounds – will vibrate a lot more.
You can even feel it for yourself – rest your fingers
at the front of your neck underneath your chin
and talk. Can you feel the vibration? Now whisper.
You'll notice that the vibration almost disappeared
completely. That's why a whisper is so quiet,
because there's so likkle vibration!

Volume gets lower as a sound-wave travels through
the air away from the source of the sound. I'm going
to give you a real-life example of how volume fades
over distance: imagine you're sat in an assembly
and you're all the way at the back, in the last row.
But a friend is all the way in the front row.
The assembly then starts, and the teacher
begins speaking. Who will hear the
teacher's voice more clearly – you, at the
back, or your friend at the front? Well, probably
your friend because they're closer to the source of
the sound, meaning that the sound-wave only has
a short distance to travel, so it doesn't spread out
and lose as much energy. But for you, the sound has
to travel a larger distance to reach you. By the time
it finally gets to you, the sound has spread out in all

WHISPERS
ARE
BARE QUIET!

directions and some of its energy was lost. This is why it would sound quieter to you.

Amplitude is a measurement of how large a sound-wave is, and it's measured from the middle of the wave to the height of its peak (the highest bit) or trough (the lowest bit). A loud sound-wave has a larger amplitude than a quiet one. The amplitude of a sound-wave – or how big it is – will affect the volume of the sound.

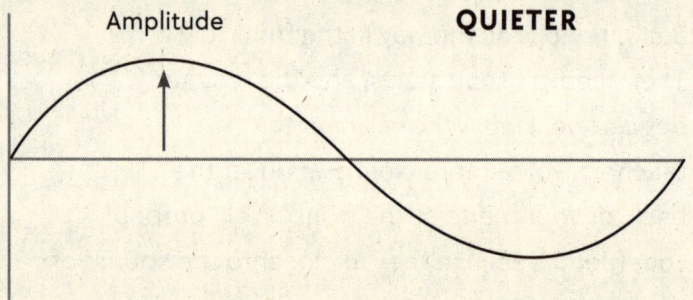

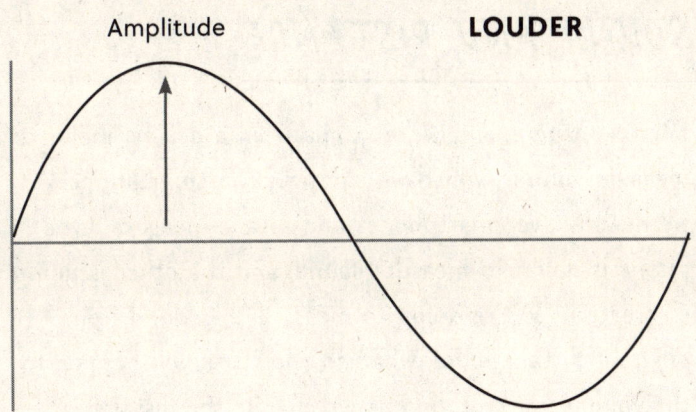

Amplitude   **LOUDER**

Right, so we know what volume is, but how do we measure it? Well, volume is measured in **decibels** (dB). I know that sounds like a mad word, but it's calm, trust me.

An exploding firework is between 150–175 decibels – that's bare loud.

But the *tick-tock* of a clock is only 20 decibels – that's a bit quiet, init.

Now, we're actually going to do an experiment to measure volume and prove that it gets quieter the farther away you are from a sound.

EXPERIMENT 11: SOUND AND DISTANCE

For this experiment, we're gonna need a decibel meter to measure volume, which we can get on a smartphone. All we need is two smartphones and a tape measure. One phone is going to measure sound, and the other is going to create it. We're going to measure the sound from different distances. So, what do you think will happen to the volume of the sound as we change the distance?

AIM: To discover if the volume of sound decreases or increases over distance.

HYPOTHESIS: I think that the sound will become quieter as we move further away from it, and become louder as we get closer.

Equipment:
★ two smartphones — one to play a song through the speaker, and the other to measure the volume of the sound.
★ a tape measure

METHOD

1. Play some music on the phone.

2. Stand directly next to the phone and use the second phone to measure the decibel level.

3. Record your results in the table below.

4. Use the tape measure to measure a one metre distance and record the decibel level from there.

5. Repeat at a distance of two, three, four and five metres.

RESULTS

DISTANCE (m)	DECIBELS (dB)
0	
1	
2	
3	
4	
5	

CONCLUSION

We can see that the decibel reading, which tells us the volume of the music, decreased as we increased our distance from the source of the sound (phone). This is because soundwaves lose energy the farther away they get from the source of the sound. **BOOM!** Sound-wave tings.

EVALUATION

What went well during this experiment? Is there anything you would do differently next time? How about trying the experiment again with a few different sounds, like using your voice or banging a drum, to compare your results? Obviously it's hard to keep your controls the same with those kind of noises though, fam, but try to keep your voice at a similar volume each time, or bang the drum with the same force.

Ite cool, I hope this chapter sounded good to you! Now you know all about sound, pitch and volume. So, the next time you're listening to a sound, like music for example, have a think about what you notice – is the sound loud or quiet, high-pitched or low-pitched? **NICE ONE, FAM!**

Here's a quick reminder of the key points we learned in this chapter:

★ Sound is produced by an object vibrating.

★ A sound-wave is the movement of energy through a medium (in other words, the stuff the sound is travelling through!).

★ Sound can travel through solids, liquids and gases.

★ The speed of sound is affected by how tightly packed together the particles in a medium are.

★ Long sound-waves have a lower pitch than short sound-waves.

★ The pitch of a sound can be measured in hertz.

★ Volume is how loud or quiet a sound is and is measured in decibels.

★ The volume of a sound decreases over distance.

CHAPTER 4
LIGHTEN UP

OK, let's lighten things up a bit! **But what exactly is light?**

Well, for starters, look at that bulb hanging from your ceiling. Or just go outside in the daytime and look up at the sky (hopefully the Sun is out!). Or maybe have a look at some candles glowing on a birthday cake. These are all **light sources**.

A light source produces light. Some sources of light are so bright that they can damage our eyes if we look directly at them. The Sun is bare bright, which is why we need to cover our eyes with sunglasses to protect them from the Sun's rays (and NEVER look at it directly).

Light is another type of energy that travels in waves. But remember how we said that a sound-wave is nothing like a wave in the ocean? Well, light waves are the opposite – they actually do move a bit like ocean waves, going up and down, up and down as they travel forward.

105

CHAPTER 4

LIGHT WAVE

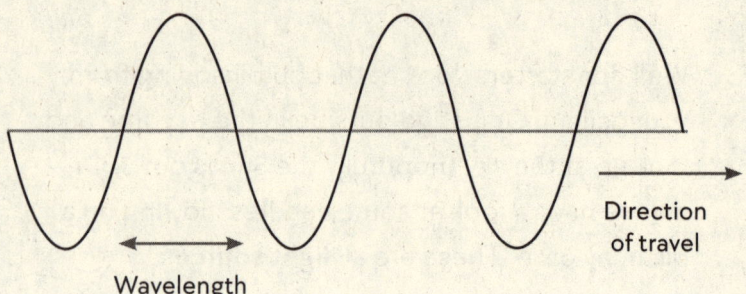

Direction of travel

Wavelength

Light always travels in straight lines, and it also travels faster than anything else in the entire universe! It travels even faster than sound, and sound is bare fast. **Light travels at 670,616,629 mph.**

THAT'S 670 MILLION MPH! OH MY DAYS, THAT IS MAD! THERE'S LITERALLY NOTHING FASTER THAN THAT.

BRILLIANT LIGHT

CHARACTERISTICS
Light-hearted and
lightning fast –
light is the fastest
thing in the universe!

GOOD AT
Lighting up a room –
and I mean literally,
fam!

LOVES
Having a good time
and celebrating!
We use light in lots
of celebrations, from
fireworks at New Year's
Eve, Diwali and Bonfire
Night, to birthday
candles!

CHAPTER 4

ILLUMINATE ME!

Light is literally everywhere, which is a good thing, because we need it to see! **The only way we can see an object is if it is illuminated, which basically means lit up – either by its own light or by reflected light.** Objects that produce – or emit – their own light are called **LUMINOUS**, and those that don't are called **NON-LUMINOUS**. We've already mentioned a few examples of luminous objects: a light bulb, the Sun and birthday candles. Other examples could be a torch or a phone screen.

Even some animals can produce their own light, which is crazy! Have you seen *Finding Nemo*? The illuminated fish in that film actually exists in real life – it's called an anglerfish. They use that glowing bobble on their head to attract prey for their dinner. Another example of animals creating their own light are fireflies. These insects have a glowing abdomen that they use to communicate with each other. Animals that give off their own light are called **bioluminescent**.

MAD COOL!

Non-luminous objects do not give off their own light – instead, they reflect light. For example, this book that you're reading is a non-luminous object. It's reflecting light from your surroundings – that could be sunlight if you're reading outside, or a light bulb if you're reading indoors.

HOW DOES LIGHT ALLOW US TO SEE?

OK, to explain how light lets us see stuff, let's imagine that we have a light source, like a torch, for example. When we shine the torch at a white wall, the light will be reflected towards us. Reflected is just another way of saying bounced back. When light is reflected, it changes direction. It's the same thing that would happen if you threw a tennis ball at a wall – it would bounce back towards you. The light does the same thing and is reflected back to you.

This reflected light then hits your eye and goes straight into it through the clear, dome-shaped surface at the front called the **cornea**. From the cornea, the light travels into your **pupil** – the black bit at the centre of your eye. The **iris** – the coloured bit of your eye – can make the pupil go bigger or smaller to control how much light enters it. When the pupil is bigger, more light enters, and when it's smaller, less light enters. Our pupils go big in the dark because we want to let in as much light as possible. In sunlight, our pupils go smaller because there's plenty of light available.

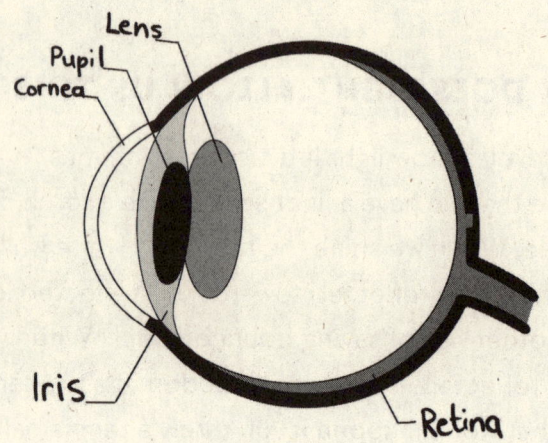

US HUMANS AREN'T VERY GOOD AT SEEING IN THE DARK UNFORTUNATELY, WHICH IS KINDA SAD, BECAUSE IT WOULD BE COOL IF WE HAD NIGHT VISION! SOME ANIMALS, LIKE CATS, DOGS AND FROGS, CAN SEE REALLY WELL IN THE DARK. IT'S BECAUSE THEY HAVE MORE CELLS IN THEIR EYES THAT CAN DETECT LIGHT.

Once light has entered the pupil, the **lens** – a clear, semicircular-shaped structure inside the eye – changes the direction of the light and focuses it on to our **retina**, the layer at the back of our eye that's sensitive to light. When the light first hits the retina, the image that we see is actually upside down! The light-sensitive cells in the retina then send a signal to the brain, which turns the image the right way up.

NOW YOU SEE ME, NOW YOU DON'T

However, not all surfaces are reflective, and this can depend on their colour and texture. Some actually absorb the light – a bit like it's being sucked in instead of bounced back! For example, black surfaces aren't very reflective. If we shine a torch at a piece of black fabric, most of the torch's light would be absorbed and not much would be reflected. Shiny, smooth, light-coloured surfaces reflect light, whereas dull, dark, rough surfaces absorb it.

EXPERIMENT 12:
A BALL OF LIGHT

Ask a grown-up to help you with this one!

OK, next we're gonna do a quick experiment to show how light is reflected and absorbed by different surfaces. For this one, all we need is a tennis ball, a wall and an old bedsheet. We're gonna first throw the tennis ball at the wall, and then at the sheet and see what happens. This time I'm not gonna give you a hypothesis, so add your own below!

AIM: To investigate how different surfaces affect how a tennis ball is reflected.

HYPOTHESIS: Write down what you think will happen here:

_____

Equipment:
* ★ an old bedsheet
* ★ some pegs and a washing line, or two chairs
* ★ a tennis ball
* ★ a wall

METHOD

1. Hang up your bedsheet outside. You could attach it to a washing line using pegs, or stretch it out between two chairs. (Please ask a grown-up first and make sure you're using an old sheet in case it gets damaged.)

2. First, throw the ball at the wall. (Make sure there's nothing else nearby — like a window! — that could get broken if you hit it.)

3. Then throw the ball into the sheet. (Throw it gently so you don't pull the sheet down!)

4. Observe what happens each time.

RESULTS

When we threw it at the wall, the tennis ball bounced back. But when we threw it at the sheet, the ball got caught up in the sheet and slowed down.

CONCLUSION

In this experiment, the wall represents a smooth, reflective surface that light can bounce off. If we imagine the tennis ball is a ray of light, we can see how the light ray hits the reflective surface and bounces straight back. The bedsheet represents a rough, non-reflective surface that absorbs light. We can see how when the light (represented by the tennis ball) hit the non-reflective surface, it slowed down and was absorbed instead of bouncing back.

EVALUATION

What went well in this experiment? What didn't go so well? Another thing you could try next time would be to compare bouncing a tennis ball on concrete versus bouncing it on grass.

EXPERIMENT 13: TIME TO REFLECT

OK cool, so now we're going to test the reflectivity of different surfaces using a real light source. For this experiment, we'll need a torch and some different surfaces. We'll shine the torch on a mirror, some aluminium foil, a black T-shirt, some white paper and a piece of cardboard. Which one do you think will be most reflective, and which one will be the least?

AIM: To investigate the reflectivity of different surfaces.

HYPOTHESIS: I think the order of reflectivity — from most reflective to least — will be the mirror, the aluminium foil, the white paper, the cardboard and finally, the black T-shirt.

Equipment:
★ a torch
★ a mirror
★ some aluminium foil
★ a sheet of white paper
★ some cardboard
★ a black T-shirt (if you don't have a black T-shirt, a black jumper or another black fabric item is fine too)

METHOD

1. Turn on the torch and turn off the light so the room is dark.

2. Shine the light on each material and observe whether the light is reflected (so you can see it shining in the dark) or absorbed (so you can hardly see it).

RESULTS

Our hypothesis was correct! The most reflective surface was the mirror, which reflected a lot of light back when we shone the torch on it. The black T-shirt absorbed the most light, so we could barely see it in the dark room.

CONCLUSION

Our results show us that the shiniest, smoothest surface (the mirror) reflected the most light, whereas the darkest and softest surface (the black T-shirt) reflected the least.

EVALUATION

Would you do anything differently next time? What other surfaces could you try?

IN THE SHADOWS

I know I said I was going to keep things light, but it's time to get a bit dark now. We're going to learn about shadows. So what is a shadow?

You've definitely seen a shadow before. You know when it's a bare hot day and you're chilling in the playground? If you look down at the floor, you'll see a black outline that has roughly the same shape as you. If you lift your arms, the shadow does too. If you jump, so does the shadow. It's basically a copycat – it just copies everything you do! All of us have a shadow, and it follows us everywhere we go.

Shadows are made when a light source is blocked by a person or an object. The light is either gonna be reflected or absorbed by that object, but it can't travel through it. The light can't reach the side of the object that's facing away from the light source because the object is in the way, and remember, light only travels in straight lines, so the area that the light can't reach is just dark. **This dark shape is what we call a shadow!**

There are some objects that don't block light, though – like glass windows, for example. We call these objects **transparent**, which means they allow light to pass through them. Materials that don't allow light to pass through them – such as wood or stone – are called **opaque**. And there are a few materials that let some light through and block some at the same time – we call these **translucent**. Tracing paper is translucent because you can kind of see through, but not clearly.

TIME FOR SOME SHADE

Maybe you've noticed that your shadow changes shape at different times of day? This is because the shape of the shadow depends on where the light source is in relation to the object. When you're outside, the light source is the Sun, and because the Sun will be in a different position in the sky depending on the time of day, your shadow keeps changing!

If a light source is directly above an object, then the shadow will be directly below the object. So at midday, when the Sun is overhead, your shadow will be directly below your feet and you can hardly see it.

But when the Sun is lower in the sky and the light hits you from the side, your shadow will be on the opposite side of the light source. Your shadow also becomes longer because the straight light rays are hitting the body from a different angle.

EXPERIMENT 14: MAKING SHADOWS

Let's have a go at making some of our own shadows. This experiment is super simple – all we need is a torch, a dark room and something to measure distance with. We're going to place our hands at different distances in front of the torch to see how this changes the shadows we make. Do you think the shadow will be larger when your hand is closer or farther away from the light source?

AIM: To investigate how shadows are made and the effects of distance upon them.

HYPOTHESIS: I think the closer my hand is to the light source, the larger the shadow will be. Different objects will produce different-shaped shadows.

Equipment:
★ a torch
★ a tape measure or ruler
★ a number of different objects, such as a coin, a fork, some leaves, or paper cut-out shapes

METHOD

1. Turn on the torch and switch off the lights.

2. Ask someone to shine the torch at a wall from about 3 m (using your ruler or tape measure to judge the distance).

3. Place your hand in front of the torch, about 50 cm from the wall.

4. Observe the shadow on the wall.

5. Gradually move your hand away from the wall towards the torch, and observe how the shadow changes.

6. Place other objects in front of the torch and observe the shape of their shadows.

RESULTS

When a hand was placed in front of the torch, a shadow formed on the wall. When the hand was closer to the torch, the shadow was larger. When the hand was farther away from the torch, the shadow was smaller.

CONCLUSION

Our hypothesis was correct! Objects that are closer to
a light source will block more light and create bigger
shadows, whereas objects that are farther away will block
less light and create smaller shadows. Larger objects will
also create bigger shadows than smaller ones because
they block more light. So, if you put your hand in front
of the torch and then put a grown-up's hand there after,
their hand would cast a bigger shadow than yours!

EVALUATION

Is there anything you would do differently next time?
Perhaps you could use your ruler or tape measure to
measure the width of the shadow each time, along with
the distance. You could even put your results into a
line graph to show how as the distance got bigger, the
shadow got smaller.

SOUND VERSUS LIGHT!

ITE, BOOM! We've spoken quite a lot about sound
and light waves. Now let's compare them and find
out more about the differences between them. We
know that sound needs a medium such as air to be
able to travel, which is why there's no sound in a
vacuum. But light, on the other hand, doesn't need
any medium to travel through. Light can still shine
even in a vacuum. This means that light can travel
through space, which is why we can see light from
stars and the Sun! Light can travel through water too,
but it's a bit slower than when it's in air or a vacuum.
In water, light travels at 500,000,000 (500 million)
mph. (That still sounds pretty fast to me, fam!)

Sound can travel through any medium, whether
it's a gas, liquid or solid. But light can only travel
through gases, liquids and some solids. For light to
be able to travel through a solid, it must be either
transparent (like glass), or translucent (like tracing
paper). Light can't travel through solids that are
opaque, like wood.

And remember what I said earlier about how
sound-waves and light waves move differently? A
light wave moves a bit like an ocean wave – up and

down – while a sound wave moves more like a slinky – forward and back. A more scientific way of saying this is that light travels in **transverse waves**, and sound travels in **longitudinal waves**.

TRANSVERSE WAVE

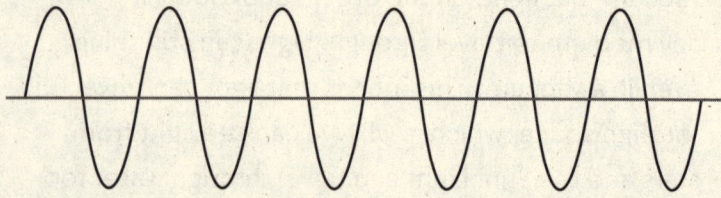

LONGITUDINAL WAVE

We detect light with our eyes, but also with cameras – which use light to capture an image. And we can detect sound with our ears, as well as microphones – which can record sounds so that they can be played back. We produce light with light bulbs, and we produce sound with speakers. Now, these devices are all powered by electricity – so I think it's time we learned a bit more about electricity, yeah?

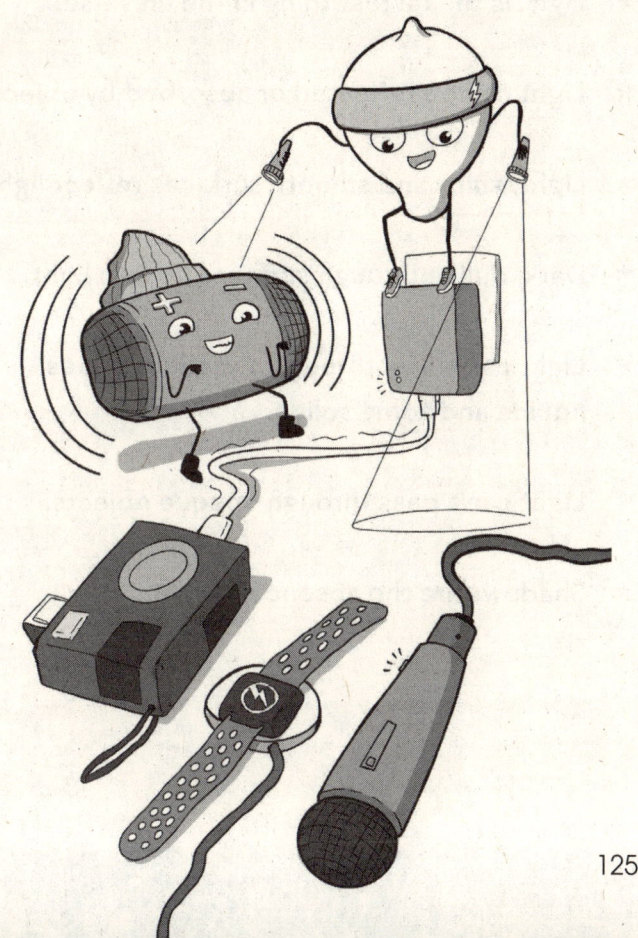

But before we move on, let's recap our key points from this chapter:

★ Luminous objects produce their own light.

★ Non-luminous objects reflect light from light sources.

★ Light is the fastest thing in the universe.

★ Light can be reflected or absorbed by objects.

★ Light, shiny and smooth surfaces reflect light.

★ Dark, dull and rough surfaces absorb light.

★ Light can travel through a vacuum, gases, liquids and some solids.

★ Light can't pass through opaque objects.

★ Shadows are the absence of light.

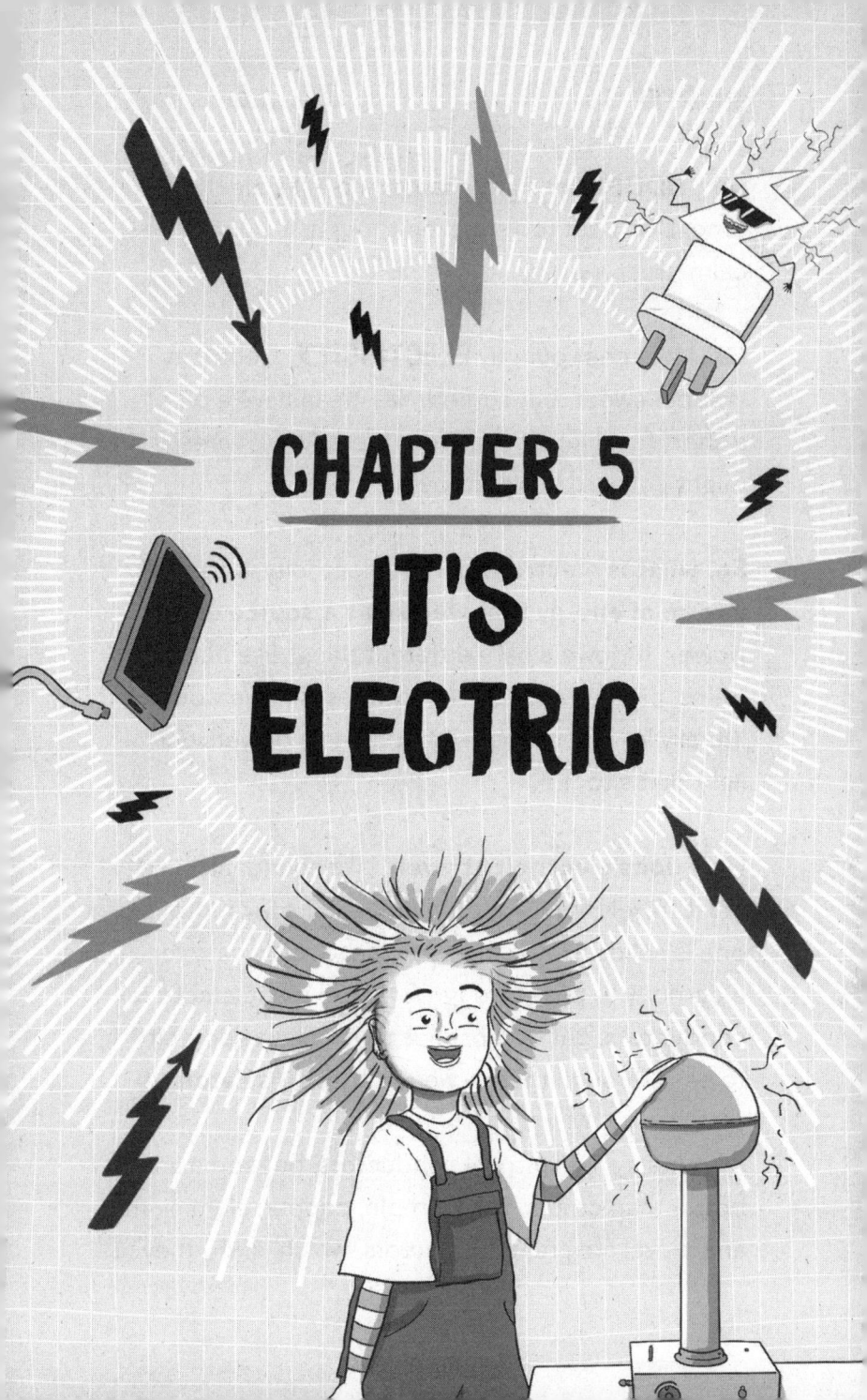

CHAPTER 5

IT'S ELECTRIC

CHAPTER 5

ITE, BOOM! Let's get charged up – it's electricity time. Don't get too shocked though; it's gonna be calm, trust me.

OK, let's meet our guy **ELECTRICITY**. Electricity is super sweet, but sometimes it can have a bit of a short fuse! And if you cross electricity's wires, it might get a likkle bit jumpy . . .

So, what is electricity? Well electricity is basically **a form of energy that we use as a source of power**. It powers bare different things like batteries, trains, phones and loads of other stuff. We would literally be in darkness without it as it powers our light bulbs too!

How does electricity travel? Like sound, electricity must travel through a medium, and its favourite one is solids. Now, some solids are really easy for electricity to pass through – we call these **electrical conductors**. But other solids don't allow electricity to pass through them – we call these **insulators**.

All metals are electrical conductors, but some are better than others. For example, copper, aluminium and nickel are great conductors, which is why they're used to make electrical wires. I'm ninety-nine per cent sure if you look around wherever you are right now, you'll probably see a wire or two. Gold is a great conductor too, but it's bare expensive, so it's rarely used to make wires (the same goes for silver). However, small amounts of gold are used in **electrical circuits** to connect the different parts. A basic electrical circuit is made up of wires, a power source and the device that you're powering – such as a light bulb.

AWESOME ELECTRICITY

LOVES
Getting lit!
(Electricity can be
converted into light.)

GOOD AT
Connecting with others –
electric circuits connect
different devices.

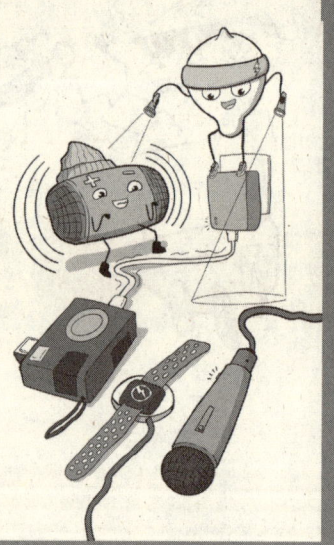

CHARACTERISTICS
A bright spark –
electricity creates
sparks – you done know!

IT'S GETTING LIT!

Ask your parent or guardian for a new light bulb and look at it. Can you see that curly-wurly coil inside? That's a **filament**, and it's made from a metal called **tungsten**. Now tungsten is an absolute MAD ting. It has the highest melting point of any metal in the entire world – 3,422° Celsius. That's over half the temperature of the Sun's surface! Oh my days.

OK, so when we turn on a light bulb, electricity passes through the tungsten coil and heats it up, I mean it gets *proper* hot. Electricity is converted into heat and light energy, and and the tungsten coil glows bright. That's how we get light, init.

NEVER TOUCH A LIGHT BULB WHEN IT IS ON, AS IT'S SUPER HOT!

Sometimes the electricity can cause the temperature of the filament to reach over 3,000° Celsius. That's why tungsten metal is used, because most other metals would just melt into a liquid at this temperature, but tungsten stays solid. That's crazy.

CHAPTER 5

CHARGE IT UP

Ask an adult to borrow an unplugged phone-charger wire and look at it. Can you see the metal wire inside? Of course not (unless you have X-ray vision!). All you can see is the plastic or rubber cover surrounding the wire. Now, plastic and rubber are good **insulators**, which is why they're used to cover materials that carry electricity. This covering stops us from receiving an **electric shock** when we pick up the phone charger! Other types of insulators include glass, dry wood and dry cotton.

Ite cool, we're gonna do a quick likkle activity now, yeah. Here are ten different items:

ALUMINIUM FOIL
GLASS WINDOW T-SHIRT
COIN BOOK
FORK TABLE TIN CAN
TISSUE METAL JEWELLERY
PLASTIC BOTTLE

I want you to mark up whether each one is an insulator or conductor. Once you're done, take a look at the answers on p.191 to see if you're right.

CHAPTER 5

WHAT ACTUALLY IS ELECTRICITY THOUGH?

OK, so we know that electricity travels through wires, but what exactly is it that's travelling through those wires? The answer is **electrons** – electrons are flowing through the wires. If you're a bit confused, don't worry. I've got you!

First, let's define what an electron is. An electron is a tiny particle inside an atom (remember those?!) with a negative charge. In a metal, some of the electrons can break away from their atoms and move around. It's this movement of electrons that creates the flow of electricity.

If that's still a bit tough to get your head around, then I want you to imagine you're at school and it's break time, so all the students are in the playground. Each individual student represents one electron, including you. Now imagine

CONGRATULATIONS, YOU'RE OFFICIALLY AN ELECTRON!

there's a running track surrounding everyone in the playground. This track represents the wires. When all the students are standing still, this means that the electrons aren't flowing and there's no electricity. When the students run around the track in the same direction, this represents electrons flowing through the wires. The flow of electrons is electricity.

The next big question is, where do you think these likkle excited electrons come from? Well, we need a power source, like a battery. Now remember, the main components – or parts – of the electric circuit are the wires, the device that you're powering (also called the **load**), and the power supply. (There are other components too, but we're gonna get into that in a bit!) Without a power supply, electricity cannot flow round the circuit.

In a simple circuit, a battery is the electrical component that provides the power source. Grab yourself an AA or AAA battery (ask an adult first!) and look at the labelling on the side. Can you see a likkle positive and negative symbol on either end? That's the positive and negative terminals.

Now, do you remember what charge an electron has? That's right – it's negative. And negative charges **REPEL** each other (in other words, try and get away from each other!), while positive and negative charges **ATTRACT** each other. So our negatively charged electrons flow away from the negative terminal of the battery and towards the positive terminal.

Wait one second. Is electricity defo going from negative to positive? I thought it was the other way around? A-ha – now this is the confusing part. When scientists first discovered electricity, they actually thought it was flowing the other way – from positive to negative. Now we know that the electrons flow the other way, but the idea stuck, and you'll still see that *current* is shown as flowing from positive to negative on circuit diagrams. This is called **conventional current**. Kinda confusing, I know, fam! But let's not stress it too much.

Electricity is pushed out through the negative terminal of the battery. It then travels round the circuit and re-enters the battery through the positive terminal. This flow of electrons is pushed by the battery.

If we go back to our imaginary playground, picture all the students (our electrons) lined up at the starting line on the track, ready to race. The starting line represents the negative terminal of the battery, where electrons leave from. No one is moving yet, as everyone's waiting for the teacher to begin the race. The teacher then shouts 'go', and the students begin to flow round the track. As everyone's running, the teacher's cheering and encouraging everyone in the race. In this case, the teacher would be the battery who starts the race and pushes the electrons around the circuit so electricity can flow. The students then run round the track, and everyone gets to the finish line to meet the teacher at the end of the race. The finish line represents the positive terminal where electrons re-enter the battery.

So how fast does electricity move? I'll tell you what, it's actually pretty fast. To see how fast, flick on a light switch. How long did it take for the bulb to light up? It's almost instant, because electricity travels at about half the speed of light. That's about 350,000,000 mph. So that's 35 million miles per hour, which is bare fast.

CHAPTER 5

SWITCH IT UP

Ite cool, we know about batteries, so now I'm gonna introduce you to the next component of our circuit – this one's called a switch. Think about that light switch I just asked you to flick on the previous page. The job of the switch is to break the circuit and stop the flow of electricity. Switches do this by creating a gap in a circuit. When a switch is on, there's no gap, the circuit is complete and the electrons can flow all the way round. When the switch is off, there's a gap and the circuit is incomplete.

So imagine you're back in the playground and you and your electron buddies are running round the track. Suddenly, a big wall blocks your way!

This forces everyone to stop running and the race stops. This is exactly what a switch does – it breaks the circuit so no electricity electricity can flow.

HIGH VOLTAGE!

You know we can measure the amount of electricity flowing through a circuit, right? One of the ways we measure it is in **volts** (V). Volts are a unit of voltage, which is basically the 'push' that makes the electricity flow round the circuit. If we wanted to increase the voltage in a circuit, there are two ways we could do it – either by replacing the battery with one of a higher voltage, or adding a second battery. A higher voltage means a greater push of electrons. Why would we want to increase the voltage? Well, circuits with lots of components need a higher voltage because more electrical energy needs to be pushed to them. So let's say we had lots of light bulbs in our circuit – we would need a higher voltage to power them all. Or perhaps we've got another type of component in our circuit – for example, a buzzer, which makes a loud buzzing sound when electricity flows through it. A higher voltage would make the light bulb brighter and the buzzer louder.

CHAPTER 5

STATIC ELECTRICITY

OK cool, so do you want to see some electricity in action? We're going to make some static electricity! Static electricity is proper easy to make – you just need to grab two objects and rub them together. As you rub them, the electrons will be transferred from one object to the other. The object that receives the electrons gets a negative electrical charge. The object that loses the electrons gets a positive electrical charge.

I'll give you a quick lesson on where these charges come from: in our atom we have **protons**, which have a positive charge, **neutrons**, which have no charge; and electrons, which have a negative charge. An atom with more protons than electrons will have a positive charge, and an atom with more electrons than protons will have a negative charge. Atoms that have the same number of protons and electrons will have no charge, or we can also say they are neutral. **BOOM!**

OK, back to static electricity. After you've rubbed it against something else, the negatively charged object now has extra electrons, and when it touches something that's neutral or positively charged, it releases all of those extra electrons really quickly. This quick release of electrons is what we call an electric shock. The negatively charged electrons are attracted to neutral or positive objects because positive and negatives attract.

YOU DONE KNOW.

Have you ever touched a stationary car and you got a likkle electric shock? Hopefully not, because it's bare painful still. But that shock is because of static electricity that has built up on the car during driving. The air rubs against the metal of the car when it's moving, which creates air resistance (remember, air resistance is when there is friction between an object and air). This transfers electrons from the air to the car, and the car gets a negative electrical charge. When you touch the car, all of these extra electrons get transferred to your body because you have a neutral charge. That's why you might feel a shock!

EXPERIMENT 15: BENDING WATER!

ITE, BOOM! So, for this experiment, we're going to add an electrical charge to a plastic comb by rubbing it against our hair. Then we're going to put the comb next to some water running from a tap. But first things first — we need that hypothesis, init. What do we think will happen to the water when we put the electrically charged object next to the running tap? Will it attract or repel the water?

AIM: To find out how static electricity affects water.

HYPOTHESIS: I think the electrically charged comb will
_____ the water.

> Equipment:
> ★ a tap
> ★ a plastic comb (or you can also use a blown-up balloon!)

METHOD

1. Rub the comb (or balloon) against your head for thirty seconds.

2. Turn on the tap.

3. Put the comb/balloon next to the stream of water and observe what happens.

RESULTS

The running water bent towards the electrically charged comb/balloon.

CONCLUSION

Was your hypothesis correct, fam? If you said the comb would attract the water, nice one!

When the comb was rubbed against your hair, electrons were transferred from the hair to the comb. The comb then got a negative electrical charge as it had more electrons. Water molecules have both a positive end and a negative end, like the poles of a magnet. The positive end of the water molecule was attracted to the negatively charged comb because positive and negative attract. So, the water bent towards the comb!

EVALUATION

Is there anything you could have done differently in this experiment? If you repeated the experiment, it would be important to make sure you kept the water temperature the same – that's our control, init.

EXPERIMENT 16:
SEE ME ROLLING!

Here's another quick static electricity experiment. For this one, we just need two items of equipment: a balloon and an empty drink can. Complete the hypothesis by circling what you think will happen.

AIM: To discover how static electricity affects a metal drink can.

HYPOTHESIS: I think the can will roll away from / towards the balloon.

Equipment:
★ a balloon
★ an empty drink can

METHOD

1. First, blow up your balloon (or get an adult to help you).

2. Then rub the balloon on your head for thirty seconds to build up an electrostatic charge.

3. With the can laying down on its side, put the balloon near the can and observe what happens.

RESULTS

You'll see that the can begins to roll as it's being attracted by the negative electrostatic charge on the balloon! Mad ting.

CONCLUSION

Was your hypothesis right this time? Yeah, I think you're getting the hang of this static electricity stuff now! The balloon got a negative charge once you rubbed it against your head. So when the balloon was placed near the drink can, the neutral atoms in the can were attracted to the negatively charged balloon. **BOOM!**

EXPERIMENT 17: FEELING ECSTATIC

Ask a grown-up to help you with this one!

Let's say we had an object, and we wanted to find out if it had a static charge or not. How would we do it? Well, we could measure it using an electroscope. An electroscope is a simple device that we can use for detecting electrical charge. It was actually first invented in the year 1600 – mad ting! Here's how we can make our own electroscope.

AIM: To measure electrostatic force.

Equipment:
★ a clear plastic cup
★ some aluminium foil
★ a paper clip
★ a comb or balloon

METHOD

1. Cut two small teardrop-shaped pieces of aluminium foil: one measuring about 1–2 cm and the other around 4–5 cm long. These are the leaves of the electroscope.

2. Straighten a paper clip and use it to poke a hole into the bottom of the clear plastic cup. (Ask an adult to help with this step.)

3. Bend one end of the paper clip into a hook shape.

4. Use the hook to gently poke a hole through the two aluminium strips and hang them so they dangle freely.

5. Push the other end of the paper clip through the hole in the plastic cup and bend the opposite end so that the foil leaves dangle inside the cup. This is your electroscope!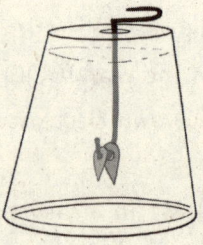

6. Place the electroscope on a flat surface.

7. Rub a comb on your head to build up charge, then put it near the paper clip at the top of the electroscope. (You could do this with an inflated balloon too.)

8. Observe what happens.

9. Try it with other electrically charged objects.

RESULTS

When the charged comb was brought near the paper clip, the foil leaves moved, which tells us the comb has a static charge.

CONCLUSION

So why did the foil leaves move then? Well, this is because the comb transferred its electrons to the paper clip and down to the foil. Since both leaves get the same charge, they repel each other — because charges that are the same (or like charges) repel each other. The greater the static charge, the more the leaves will repel each other and move. This is how an electroscope tells us how much static electricity an object has!

EVALUATION

How did this experiment go? Did you try it with a few different types of electrically charged objects? What did you notice, and how could you do it differently next time?

ELECTRICITY = ENERGY!

OK, so we know electricity can be converted into light (remember our light bulb?), but can it turn into any other forms of energy? Yes, it can!

Electricity can be converted into **HEAT ENERGY** – for example, in electric cookers and heaters. In electric heaters, you have something called a heating element: this is made of metal and is often a coil or tube shape. When electrons travel through the heating element, they crash into the metal atoms inside it. These collisions cause the electrons to lose energy in the form of heat, which transfers to the metal. As a result, heat energy is produced when the electrons flow through the heating element.

Electricity can also be converted into sound – that's how speakers work, init. Man's gonna tell you how electricity transforms into a likkle sound-wave.

When electricity enters a speaker, it whizzes through a coil. But this coil is different from the one in a light bulb or heating element as it's made from a metal called copper. Now, copper is the second-best electrical conductor of all the metals in the whole world. Do you remember what an electrical conductor is? That's right – it's a material that allows electricity to pass through it. Copper can conduct electricity (allow it to pass through) really well. The only metal better at conducting electricity than copper is silver, but obviously silver's bare expensive, so we don't really use it for wires that much . . .

Anyway, back to the copper coil inside the speaker. So, electricity passes through the copper coil, and this creates what we call a **magnetic field**.

A magnetic field is an area where there is magnetic force. Imagine you're moving an iron nail closer and closer to a strong magnet – at some point, the nail's gonna jump forward and stick to the magnet. That's because the magnetic field pulls the nail towards the magnet, even when they're not touching. Magnetic fields can also be generated by a moving electric charge – in this case, the electric current that's flowing through the copper coil. (We're gonna learn some more about magnets in chapter 6!)

The copper coil is surrounded by a magnet, and the magnetic field from the coil causes the magnet to move back and forth. The magnet is attached to the speaker cone – the part of the speaker that's shaped – you guessed it! – like a cone. As the magnet moves back and forth, it pushes and pulls on the cone, which in turn pushes and pulls on the air around it. The air molecules start knocking into each other, creating a sound-wave!

BOOM - THAT'S HOW YOU GET SOUND FROM ELECTRICITY.

ELECTRICITY + MOVEMENT

Ite, so we know electricity can be converted into heat, light and sound, but what else?

Well, it can also be converted into movement – or what scientists call **KINETIC ENERGY**. You know them days when it's so hot outside that you have to pull out the fan . . . well, have you ever wondered,

how does the fan spin? Well, electricity enters the
fan and goes through – yep, you've guessed it – a
coil. You're probably thinking, *what, another coil? Are
you serious?* Coils are bare special still, I can't lie.
But yeah, electricity goes through the coil inside the
fan and generates a magnetic field, similar to what
happens in the speaker. This magnetic field interacts
with a magnet in the fan, causing the magnet to spin.
The magnet is attached to the blades of the fan, so
they spin too – creating a nice cool breeze!

Right, so now we've learned that electricity can
be converted into many different useful forms of
energy. My favourite is heat energy because it cooks
my tasty food!

EXPERIMENT 18:
SEPARATING SALT AND PEPPER

It's time for another experiment! We're gonna need some salt and pepper for this one, but not for seasoning food. Instead, we're going to separate a mixture of salt and pepper using static electricity! So what we're going to do is charge up our comb again, and then use it to attract the salt or pepper. Which one do you think will be attracted to the comb? Fill in your answer by circling it in the hypothesis below.

AIM: To separate a mixture of salt and pepper using static electricity.

HYPOTHESIS: I think the salt/pepper will be attracted to the electrically charged comb.

Equipment:
★ some salt
★ some pepper
★ a teaspoon
★ a bowl
★ a comb or inflated balloon

METHOD

1. Put one teaspoon of salt and half a teaspoon of pepper in a bowl.

2. Mix them well with the spoon.

3. Sprinkle the mixture on to a flat surface.

4. Charge the comb (or balloon) by rubbing it on your head for thirty seconds.

5. Hold the charged comb just above the salt and pepper mixture.

6. Observe what happens to the mixture.

RESULTS

The electrically charged comb caused the pepper to jump, as it was attracted to the comb!

CONCLUSION

Was your hypothesis correct? Nice one, fam! So yeah, the pepper was attracted to the comb. This is because pepper is lighter than salt, so the static charge has a stronger effect on the pepper. The salt is too heavy for the static charge to pick it up very well.

EVALUATION

What went well in this experiment, and what didn't go so well? Write down your observations.

ITE, BOOM! I hope you're feeling electrified by this chapter. Now man knows all about what electricity is, how we create static electricity, and what energy forms we can convert electricity into. Let's recap some of our key points, init:

★ Electricity is measured in volts (V).

★ Electricity is the flow of electrons.

★ Electricity can be converted into heat, light, sound and kinetic energy.

★ Electricity travels through metals such as copper and tungsten.

★ A conductor allows electricity to pass through it.

★ An insulator doesn't allow electricity to pass through it.

★ An electrical circuit is made of components such as a battery, wires, a switch, a light bulb or a buzzer.

★ Static electricity is produced by rubbing two objects together.

★ Static electricity is the transfer of electrons from one object to another.

CHAPTER 6

MAD
MAGNETS

ITE COOL, now that I've pulled you in, let's get to know more about *mad magnets*. Magnets are like superheroes – they can pull objects towards them without even touching them! They're like bare popular cos things are naturally attracted to them. But magnets don't hang with just anyone, though – they're super selective about who they chill with.

Magnets are metals that attract other metals. They're made from magnetic materials such as iron, nickel, steel and cobalt. The magnet just needs to be near a metal, and it will move instantly. That's some superhero ting! This is because of something you might remember from the previous chapter – the space around the magnet, or its magnetic field, has pushing and pulling forces. Not all metals are magnetic though. For example, copper and aluminium aren't magnetic.

MARVELLOUS MAGNET

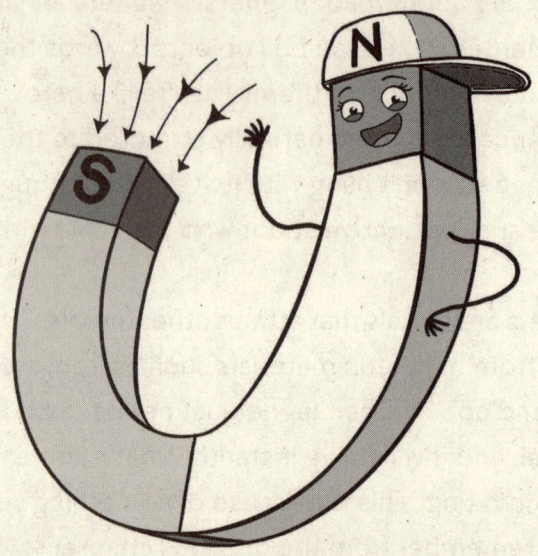

CHARACTERISTICS
Super popular
(attracts things
towards it)

LOVES
Chilling by the fridge –
fridge magnets stick to
the fridge!

GOOD AT
Sticking together –
magnets attract
each other.

Right, so first, we need to iron out a few things. **How do magnets work?** It's actually quite simple, you know. Think of a battery, which has a positive (+) and negative (-) end. Like batteries, magnets also have a positive and negative end. However, in magnets, these ends are called poles. A magnet has a north pole and a south pole.

Let's say we have two magnets. When the north pole of one magnet is put near the south pole of the other magnet, they attract each other. (Remember, attract means to pull together). So opposite poles attract each other, like two best friends who are the total opposite of each other, but they always stick together.

However, when the north pole of one magnet is put near the north pole of another, they repel each other (or push each other away). Two south poles brought together will also repel each other. So poles that are the same repel each other, like two people who are so similar that they just get on each other's nerves!

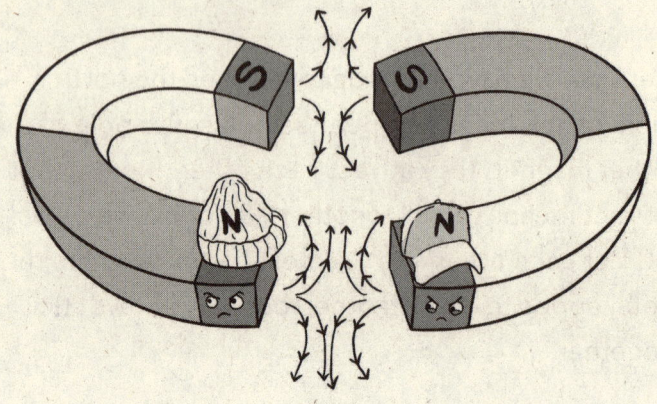

Let's look a likkle bit more at this area around the magnet called the magnetic field. When a metal enters the magnetic field, it is attracted or repelled by the magnet. A metal can only be attracted or repelled if it is within the magnetic field of the magnet. The bigger the magnet, the stronger the magnetic field. **The magnetic field surrounds the whole magnet, but it's strongest at the poles.** You can't actually see it because it's invisible to the human eye, but trust me, it's there.

If you don't believe me, you can feel the power of the magnet for yourself. All you need to do is go to the fridge and grab a fridge magnet. Put the magnet very close to the fridge, like 1 cm away. What can you feel? You should feel the magnetic field pulling the magnet towards the fridge!

Maybe you've heard of a bar magnet? Why's it called that? Well, because it looks like a bar, init. You done know. Bar magnets have a north and

LET'S TAKE A LiKKLE LOOK AT THiS BAR MAGNET TiNG.

south pole. Imagine you are a bar magnet: the north pole would be your head and the south pole would be your feet. Now I want you to stretch out your arms and legs like you're about to do a star jump. The distance your arms and legs can reach is your magnetic field. You can only attract or repel other metals if they come within reach of your magnetic field, which is the reach of your arms and legs.

YOU DONE KNOW!

CHAPTER 6

Magnets are useful because they stick things together. Like fridge magnets, for example. Or you know those heavy doors in public hallways that stay open by themselves? They're being held open by door magnets. Door magnets can have a pull force of around 40 kg, which sounds pretty strong when you compare them to a likkle fridge magnet – but these are actually still weak magnets. A strong magnet can lift much heavier objects – for example, those magnetic cranes used in scrapyards to pick up metals have a pull force of up to 40,000 kg, which means they can lift three double-decker buses at once! That's a mad ting.

Even though these crane magnets are bare strong, they still wouldn't be able to pick us up. Why? Simply because we don't have enough iron inside our bodies. Remember, magnets attract metals, and us humans are mostly made of water! Our bodies are about 60 per cent water, in fact. And it's probably a good thing that we're not magnetic, otherwise we'd get stuck to the fridge door every time we went to get a snack!

EXPERIMENT 19: WHAT'S MAGNETIC?

ITE, BOOM! Now we're gonna do a quick likkle experiment. We've got a range of different materials, and we're going to use a fridge magnet to test them and see which ones are magnetic. So first, we need a hypothesis. Which ones do you think will be magnetic, and which ones won't be?

AIM: To investigate which materials are magnetic.

HYPOTHESIS: Circle all of the things you think will be magnetic in the equipment list below.

Equipment:
- ★ a fridge magnet
- ★ a water bottle
- ★ a screw
- ★ some paper
- ★ some aluminium foil
- ★ a T-shirt
- ★ a teaspoon
- ★ a crayon
- ★ a wooden door
- ★ some coins
- ★ some keys
- ★ a fridge door

METHOD

1. Test each object individually by putting the magnet near it, and record your observations.

RESULTS

I've given you the first answers here — it's up to you to fill in the rest!

MAGNETIC	NON-MAGNETIC
Screw	Paper
Teaspoon	

CONCLUSION

We can conclude that all of the items made from metal were magnetic — apart from the aluminium foil because, as we know, aluminium isn't magnetic.

EVALUATION

Was there anything you might do differently next time? What about measuring how close you had to move the magnet before the object was attracted to it? This would tell you more about the magnet's magnetic field.

WHAT IS A COMPASS?

Ite cool, so now we know a bit about how magnets work, let's find out about some of their uses.

Have you ever used a **compass** before? I don't mean the type you use to draw circles in maths; I mean like a likkle round thing with an arrow that points north. A compass can tell us what direction we're travelling in – and it uses magnets to do this.

The arrow or needle that you see inside a compass is made from steel, which is magnetic. **This likkle needle is really stubborn, because it always points north, no matter what!** Even if you try to spin the compass round and upside down, it will still point in the same direction. But why though?

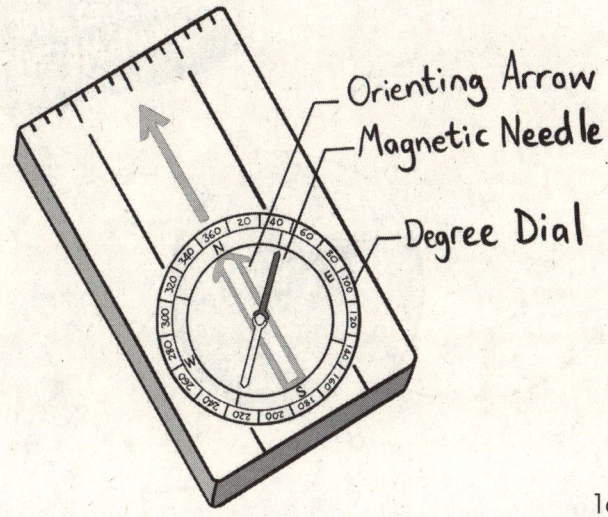

Orienting Arrow
Magnetic Needle

Degree Dial

167

Well, deep inside the centre of the Earth is an area known as the outer core, where there is loads of liquid iron metal – bare hot! As we know, iron metal is magnetic, init, so it generates a magnetic field that pulls on all of the magnetic materials on Earth – including the steel needle in the compass! And as we know, the magnetic field is strongest at the north and south pole of a magnet. If we imagine Earth as a big magnet, those poles are located at the North Pole in the Arctic and the South Pole in the Antarctic. The north pole of our magnetic compass needle is attracted to Earth's North Pole – which actually acts like the south or negative pole on a magnet.

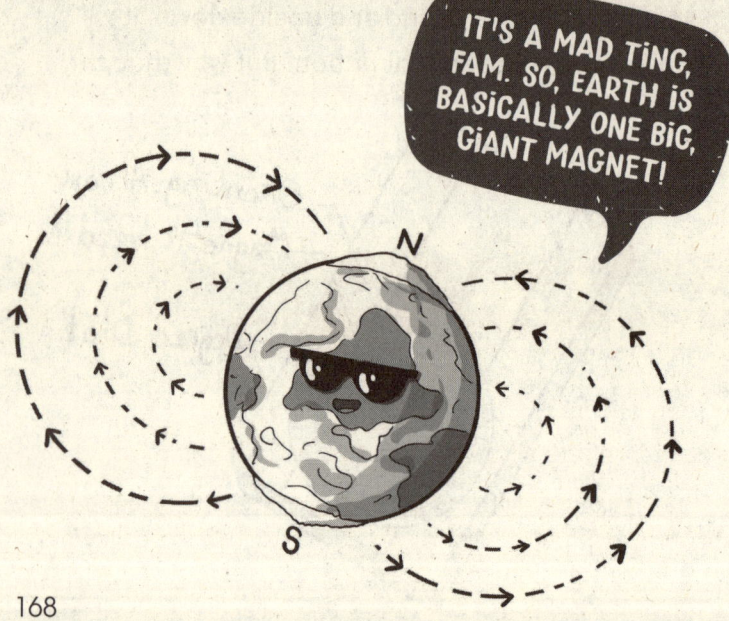

IT'S A MAD TING, FAM. SO, EARTH IS BASICALLY ONE BIG, GIANT MAGNET!

DIFFICULTY LEVEL:
Big Science

EXPERIMENT 20:
MAKE YOUR OWN COMPASS!

Ask a grown-up to help you with this one!

You know we can make our own compasses at home, right? We can do this by magnetizing a sewing needle! Which direction do you think the needle will point — east, north, south or west?

AIM: To find out how compasses are affected by Earth's magnetic field.

Equipment:
★ a sewing needle
★ a fridge magnet
★ a cork
★ a pair of scissors
★ a bowl
★ some water

HYPOTHESIS: I think the needle will point north.

METHOD

1. Magnetize the needle by moving the fridge magnet along it from one end to the other. Do this thirty times in the same direction, like when you're combing hair.

2. Cut off a coin-shaped piece from the cork. (Get an adult to help you!)

3. Pour some water into the bowl.

4. Place the cork on top of the water.

5. Carefully balance the needle on top of the cork and observe what happens.

RESULTS

The sewing needle is now magnetic and acts as a compass that point towards Earth's north!

CONCLUSION

Wow, I can't lie – this experiment is pretty cool! Moving

the fridge magnet up and down your needle made it magnetic because it caused the atoms inside the metal to all line up with their north poles facing one way. (That's right — atoms have a north and a south pole too!) The north pole of your now magnetic needle was attracted to Earth's north — which acts like the south pole on a magnet — because opposite poles attract!

EVALUATION

How could you make sure that your compass was actually facing north? You can use the compass app on a smartphone to check that your homemade compass is working properly. How accurate is your homemade compass compared to the one on the phone?

Woah, that chapter was pretty mad. I can't lie, magnets are seriously cool – they're like superheroes with how they can control stuff without actually touching anything! Let's remind ourselves of the key points we learned about magnets:

★ Magnets are made from metals such as iron, nickel, cobalt and steel.

★ The magnetic field of a magnet is strongest at its poles.

★ Opposite poles attract and like poles repel.

★ Magnets have an invisible magnetic field that pulls magnetic material towards them.

★ Compasses contain a magnetic needle that is affected by Earth's magnetic field.

★ Earth's North Pole actually acts like the south pole on a magnet, so the north pole of a magnetic compass needle is attracted to Earth's north.

ITE, BOOM! So we've had a look at some simple ting experiments, right the way up to big science ones. But when you get older, if you choose to continue studying science, you're gonna get to do some mad physics experiments! Let me introduce you to a few of them . . .

> **!** This chapter is full of awesome experiments that are NOT to be tried at home – these are just to give you a flavour of some even bigger science you might get to try when you're older, fam!

THAT'S SHOCKING!

Remember how earlier in the book you made static electricity by rubbing an object on your head to build up charge? This static electricity had quite a low voltage and current, so it wasn't enough to shock you. But what would happen if you made some static electricity that had a voltage and current that was 1,000 times higher? Woah!

This is an experiment that you might do in secondary school. It uses a machine called a **Van de Graaff generator** to make 100,000 volts!

Inside the machine is a spinning belt that rubs against a brush. Every time the belt spins, it builds up electricity that is then stored in a metal dome at the top of the machine. The longer it spins, the more electricity builds up.

There's so much electricity in the dome that if you were to put a metal conductor near it, the electricity would jump between the metals and you would see loads of sparks. It looks like mini lightning strikes!

Your teacher may even let you place your hand on the metal dome. As it is building up electricity, the electrons will be transferred to your body, and your hair will begin to stand up on its ends!

LEVEL UP

IT'S GETTING LIT

There are also some absolutely crazy experiments that can be done with light. Did you know that you can use sunlight to literally melt solid rock or even metals? This can be done by using only a lens and the Sun's rays.

A lens is a curved piece of glass used to focus light. Lenses work by changing the direction of the light and focusing it to one area. As light rays enter the lens, they're all bent towards one specific spot. This focus of light makes this spot get extremely hot – sometimes up to 1,000° Celsius! That's as hot as lava from a volcano!

RAINBOW COLOURS

This is another cool light experiment, and it's one you might do in secondary school. Have you noticed how when you look at a light bulb, or in the sunlight, the light has a white colour? Well, this 'white' isn't just one colour; it's actually made of a combination of different ones. These colours are red, orange, yellow, green, blue, indigo and violet.

THAT'S RIGHT, FAM – THESE ARE THE COLOURS OF THE RAINBOW!

Do these colours sound familiar?

Visible light is made up of all these different colours combined, but our brain perceives it as white. In order for us to see the different colours, the light needs to be split up – or **dispersed**.

We can disperse light by shining a light source through a **prism** (a glass shape with lots of different sides). The light bounces off the different sides of the prism and gets split up, so we see a rainbow of colours!

What about actual rainbows though? You might know that a rainbow usually happens when the Sun is shining through the rain. Just like light shining through a prism, the sunlight shining through the raindrops gets split up. And that's how we get a rainbow!

ICE COLD

At the start of the book, we learned that matter is anything we can touch and feel. What's the coldest thing you've ever touched? Maybe an ice cube, some frozen peas or possibly some snow? These all have a temperature of around -18° Celsius. Now that is kinda cold, but what if I told you there's

CHAPTER 7

something that is ten times colder than the ice in your fridge?

Meet liquid nitrogen. Liquid nitrogen has a temperature of -196° Celsius – that is insane! You won't find any place in the world that's as cold as liquid nitrogen. Even Antarctica isn't that cold! Anything liquid nitrogen touches instantly freezes into a stiff solid. Let's say we took a soft and delicate rose and dipped it into a cup of liquid nitrogen. What do you think would happen? All the liquid water inside the rose would instantly be frozen into ice crystals. These ice crystals

THAT'S SOME CRAZY KIND OF MATTER RIGHT THERE.

break the cells of the rose. If the rose is dropped or hit, it will immediately shatter into loads of tiny pieces.

SO MAGNETIC

Remember what I said in the magnets chapter about not being able to see a magnetic field because it's invisible? Well, when you get to secondary school, you're probably going to do an experiment that allows you to see what a magnetic field looks like!

To do this, you'll need a magnet, some iron filings (small pieces of iron) and a piece of paper. First, you'll place the piece of paper on top of the magnet. Then, you'll sprinkle some iron filings on top of the paper.

You'll notice that as soon as the iron filings touch the paper, they don't just land in any random place. They arrange themselves in a specific pattern along the magnetic field lines. The filings follow the same shape as the magnetic field around the magnet, which allows you to see what the magnetic field actually looks like!

ITE, BOOM! You've made it! You're a real scientist now. We met some cool characters like electricity, sound, magnets and light. We also found out about their personalities and compared them.

Take light, for example. It's the fastest and can beat anyone in a race – it doesn't matter whether the race is in air or water, light will win every time. The only thing that can stop it is an opaque solid. Light is the fastest thing in the whole universe.

Sound is also super quick too, especially when it's travelling through solids. But sound does get slowed down a bit by liquids and gases.

CONCLUSION

Even though sound is rapid, it's not as quick as electricity. Electricity is the second fastest after light. It moves faster than you can blink! Magnets, on the other hand, aren't really interested in running – they pull everything to them with their magnetic field.

We also had a look at how things can get a bit heated sometimes, thanks to forces like friction! Friction can either be a nuisance or really helpful, depending on the situation . . . like, when you're sliding down a slide, friction can be a bit annoying cos it slows you down. But if you needed to climb up a steep hill, the rough sole on your shoes would create friction and help you to grip.

Another cool force we looked at was air resistance, which is very important for aeroplanes. Air resistance can slow planes down when they're flying, and that's why they have a thin, long and pointy shape to reduce air resistance. Parachutes, on the other hand, are the complete opposite – they have a wide and flat shape to create as much air resistance as possible. This is because skydivers want to slow down when falling, and the more air resistance there is, the slower they fall.

By learning about these awesome forces and different types of energy, we can understand the world around us a likkle better. And that's what physics is all about!

I hope that now you feel more confident in using experiments to try out different ideas and explore how stuff works. I always say that curiosity is the key to being a great scientist, and it really is true – science is all about asking questions and being curious about the world. If you don't ask, then you'll never know!

BIG MANNY

IT'S QUIZ TIME!

OK, we're gonna practise some of the awesome science you learned in this book. Have a go at the quiz questions below, or get a friend to test you!

FORCES

1. **Fill in the sentences below by selecting one of the words in brackets at the end:**

A   A contact force happens between two objects that _____ physically touching, and a non-contact force happens between two objects that _____ physically touching. **(aren't, are)**

B   Force is measured in _____. **(Newtons, miles per hour, inches)**

C   Friction _____ the speed of an object. **(decreases, increases)**

D   Rough surfaces produce_____ friction than smooth surfaces. **(more, less)**

E   Air resistance is friction between a moving object and _____. **(air, water, sound)**

F   The larger the surface area of an object, the _____ the air resistance. **(greater, smaller)**

G   Bigger gears turn _____ than smaller gears. **(faster, slower)**

H Bigger gears produce _____ power than smaller gears. **(more, less)**

I Smaller gears turn _____ than bigger gears. **(faster, slower)**

SOUND

2. Fill in the sentences below by selecting one of the words in brackets:

A Sound is produced when an object _____. **(vibrates, floats, freezes)**

B The movement of sound energy is called a _____. **(sound-wave, air wave, ear wave)**

C A space with no air is called a _____. **(vacuum, hoover, broom)**

D The speed of sound in air is _____. **(761mph, 76mph, 7600mph)**

3. Rank these mediums in order according to how fast sound travels through them, starting with the slowest: solids, gas, liquids

1._____

2._____

3._____

4. **Are the below statements true or false?**

A Sound travels faster in solids than liquids.

B Short sound-waves cause the air to vibrate more quickly than long sound waves.

5. **What is the frequency range for human hearing?**

A 20–20,000 Hz

B 20–200 Hz

C 20–2,000 Hz

6. **Fill in the sentences below by selecting one of the words in brackets:**

A Pitch is measured in _____. **(hertz, grams, metres)**

B The _____ of a sound is how high or low it is. **(pitch, volume, colour)**

C _____ sound-waves have high pitch and _____ sound waves have low pitch. **(short, long)**

D Volume is measured in _____. **(decibels, cowbells, litres)**

E The volume of a sound _____ as it travels away from its source. **(increases, decreases)**

LIGHT

7. Fill in the sentences below by selecting one of the words in brackets:

A _____ objects produce their own light, whereas _____ objects reflect light. **(non-luminous, luminous)**

B The speed of light is _____. **(670 million mph, 67 mph, 6700 mph)**

C Dark, dull and rough surfaces _____ light, whereas shiny, smooth and light surfaces _____ light. **(reflect, absorb)**

D _____ objects allow some light through, but _____ objects allow no light through. **(translucent, opaque)**

E Light is detected by our _____. **(eyes, ears)**

8. Is the below statement true or false?
Light can travel in a vacuum.

A True

B False

9. Which material is transparent?

A wood

B glass

C cotton.

ELECTRICITY

10. **Fill in the sentences below by selecting one of the words in brackets:**

A Electricity is measured in _____. **(volts, bolts, Celsius)**

B Electricity is the flow of_____. **(waves, electrons, electromagnets)**

C _____ allow electricity to pass through. **(conductors, insulators)**

D _____ do not allow electricity to pass through. **(conductors, insulators)**

E A _____ breaks the electrical circuit. **(bulb, buzzer, switch)**

F Static electricity is produced by _____ between two objects. **(friction, attraction, conduction)**

11. **Is the below statement true or false?**
    Static electricity is the transfer of electrons from one object to another.

A True

B False

12. **Which of the below materials is the best conductor?**

A   wood

B   copper

C   wool

MAGNETS

13. **Which metal is not magnetic?**

A   copper

B   iron

C   nickel

14. **What are the ends of a magnet called?**

A   poles

B   terminals

C   sides

15. **Fill in the sentences below by selecting one of the words in brackets:**

A   Opposite poles _____ and like poles
    _____. **(repel, attract)**

B   The area surrounding a magnet is called the
    magnetic _____. **(field, pitch, ring)**

C   A compass points in the direction of _____.
    (west, south, north, east)

ANSWERS TO PAGES 132-133:

ALUMINIUM FOIL – conductor
GLASS WINDOW – insulator
T-SHIRT – insulator
COIN – conductor
BOOK – insulator
FORK – conductor
TABLE – insulator
TIN CAN – conductor
TISSUE – insulator
METAL JEWELLERY – conductor
PLASTIC BOTTLE – insulator

ANSWERS TO PAGES 184-191:

1.
  A. are, aren't
  B. Newtons
  C. decreases
  D. more
  E. air
  F. slower
  G. more
  H. faster
  I. slower

2.
  A. vibrates
  B. sound-wave
  C. vacuum
  D. 761mph

3.
   1. gas
   2. liquids
   3. solids

4.
   A. True
   B. True

5.
   A. 20–20,000 hZ

6.
   A. hertz
   B. pitch
   C. Short, long
   D. decibels
   E. decreases

7.
   A. luminous, non-luminous
   B. 670 million mph
   C. absorb, reflect
   D. translucent, opaque
   E. eyes

8.
   A. True

9.
  B. glass

10.
  A. volts
  B. electrons
  C. conductors
  D. insulators
  E. switch
  F. friction

11.
  A. True

12.
  B. wool

13.
  A. copper

14.
  A. poles

15.
  A. attract, repel
  B. field
  C. north

YOU GOT THIS, FAM!

HOW TO FOLD A PAPER PLANE
STANDARD

1.

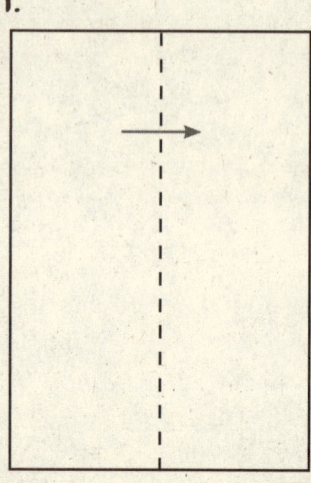

2.

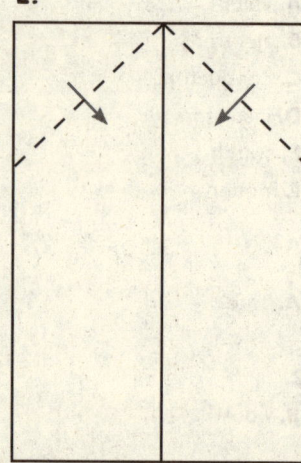

3.

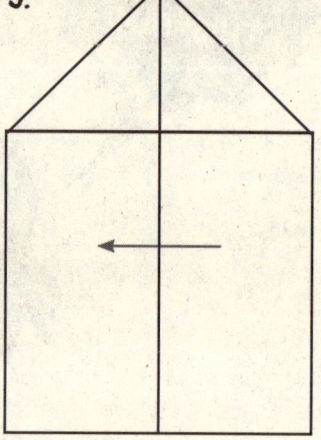

4.

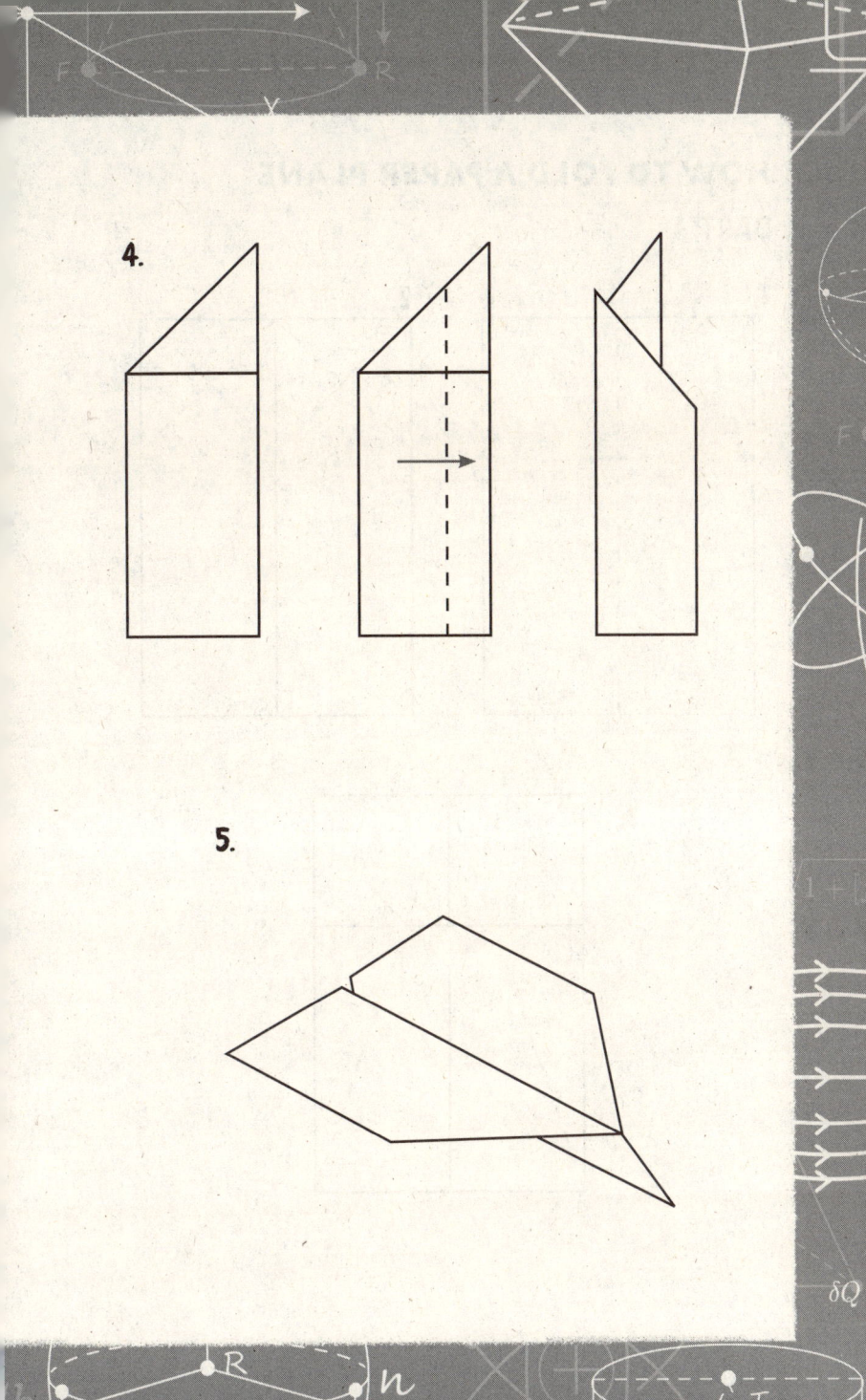

5.

HOW TO FOLD A PAPER PLANE
DART

1.

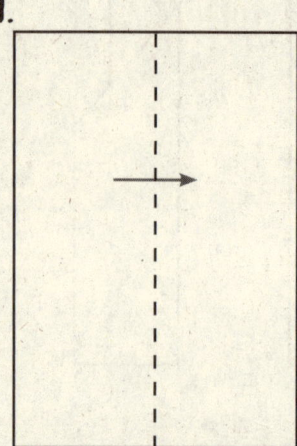

2.

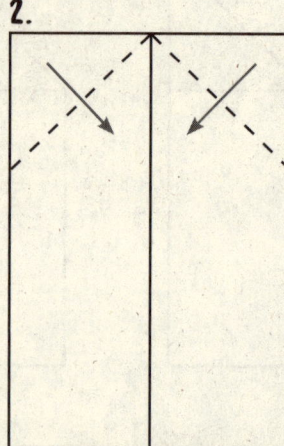

3.

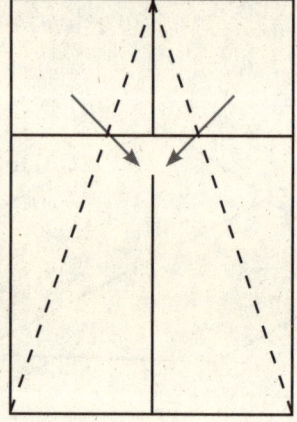

4.

5.

air resistance: a force that slows an object down as it moves through a gas. It acts in the opposite direction to the one in which the object is travelling.

amplitude: the measurement of how much energy a wave has in metres. On a waveform, amplitude is the distance from the centre line to the top of a crest or bottom of a trough.

atom: the smallest building blocks that make up everything. All elements are made from atoms.

bioluminescence: the release of light by living organisms through biochemical reactions.

cochlea: a hollow, spiral-shaped tube in the ear that looks like a snail shell. It receives sound and changes it into nerve signals, which are then sent to the brain.

GLOSSARY

compass: a device that contains a magnetized needle that swings freely on a pivot. The needle always points north.

conventional current: the flow of electrical current in a circuit from the positive terminal to the negative terminal.

cornea: the clear, dome-shaped outer layer of the eye that covers and protects the iris and pupil.

Correlation: a relationship or connection between two things. Changing one thing causes a change in the other.

cross-referencing: looking up information in more than one place and comparing the different sources of information to find connections and similarities. This makes research more reliable.

decibels: the measurement of the loudness of a sound.

disperse: to spread something out and scatter it in different directions.

ear drum: a thin, stretchy layer deep inside the ear that vibrates when hit by sound-waves. These vibrations are then sent to the brain.

echo: a sound that is bounced back to you after you make it.

effort: the work or energy you put into doing something.

electrical circuit: a path (usually along wires) that an electrical current flows through to power electrical components such as lights, speakers or motors.

electrical conductor: a material that easily allows electricity or heat to pass through it.

electric shock: an uncomfortable feeling caused by electricity passing through your body. It's usually caused by touching something that has an electrical current.

electromagnetic spectrum: the range of all the different types of electromagnetic waves that exist. Some of these waves are visible (including light) and some are invisible (such as x-rays). The waves all have different lengths.

electrons: tiny, negatively charged particles that move around the centre of an atom.

energy: the thing that makes things move. Comes in different forms such as heat, sound or light.

filament: a thin, tiny wire inside a light bulb that gets extremely hot and glows bright when electricity flows through it.

fixed axle: an axle that does not move. It stays in one place while the wheels turn around it.

flammable: catches fire easily

friction: a force that slows a moving object down when rubbing against another object. Friction acts in the opposite direction to the one the object is travelling in.

fulcrum: the support point or pivot where a lever rests and moves on. On a see-saw, the fulcrum is the middle point that the bar is balanced on.

GLOSSARY

gas: a type of matter. Unlike solids and liquids, gases do not have a fixed shape or volume, which means they can spread far apart to fill the entire space they're in. Particles in a gas are packed loosely together.

Hertz: the unit of measurement for the frequency of a sound. It measures how many vibrations occur in a sound per second. For example, a sound with a frequency of 100 Hz is vibrating 100 times in a second.

insulator: a material that does not allow electricity or heat to pass through it easily.

iris: the coloured part of the eye that controls how much light gets in. In bright conditions, the iris makes the hole that light enters through (the pupil) smaller to protect the eye. In the dark, the iris makes the pupil bigger to allow in more light.

lens: the clear, curved structure inside the eye that focuses incoming light. The lens changes its shape, which changes the direction of light entering the eye to focus an image.

light source: anything that produces light so we can see (for example, the Sun, light bulbs, a campfire).

linkage: when two or more things are connected or joined together to work as one unit.

liquid: a state of matter that flows and takes the shape of its container. Liquids can be poured but have a fixed volume. They do not spread far apart like gases. Particles in liquids are packed together more tightly than in gases but less than in solids.

load (circuits): a part of an electrical circuit that uses electrical energy to function (e.g. a light bulb, buzzer or motor). It converts electrical energy into other forms such as light, sound or movement.

load (levers): the object that a lever is trying to lift or move. It's the thing that effort is applied to.

longitudinal wave: a type of wave where particles in the medium (solid, liquid,, gas) are moving back and forth in the same direction as the wave is travelling. It's similar to a train that is moving forward while rocking back and forth.

magnetic field: an invisible area surrounding a magnet or electrical current where magnetic forces can be felt. Magnets are either attracted or repelled when they enter a magnetic field.

magnetism: the force that makes magnetic objects such as metals attract or repel each other. It's caused by the movement of electrons inside atoms.

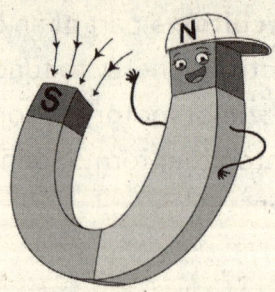

matter: anything that takes up space and has a mass. Matter makes up air, water, the Earth and the human body.

medium: a material or substance that allows waves to travel through it to carry energy. The medium can be solids, liquids or gases. The waves could be sound or light.

molecule: when two or more atoms join (or bond) together, a molecule is formed. An oxygen molecule (O_2) is made from two single oxygen atoms bonding together.

neutron: a tiny particle found in the nucleus (centre) of an atom. It has no electrical charge and is neutral.

newton: the unit of measurement for the amount of force. It measures how hard something is being pushed or pulled.

GLOSSARY

opaque: objects or materials that do not allow light to pass through.

ossicles: three tiny bones inside the middle ear that carry sound vibrations to the inner ear. They're the smallest bones in the human body.

pie chart: a type of graph that displays data in a circle. Each slice of the circle represents a part of the whole. The size of the slice shows how much that part contributes to the whole.

pitch: how high or low a sound is. Pitch depends on the frequency of the sound. A high frequency has a high pitch and a low frequency a low pitch.

prism: a solid, three-dimensional object that has all flat sides and two identical ends. It's often made from glass or clear plastic, and is used to split light into different colours by refraction.

proton: a tiny particle found in the nucleus (centre) of an atom. It has a positive charge.

pupil: the black circular opening in the centre of your iris that light passes through. The pupil size changes depending on how much light is available, and this is controlled by the iris.

Radio wave: a type of electromagnetic wave that carries energy through air. It has a long wavelength and is used to carry TV, radio and mobile-phone signals through air.

reflect: to bounce back from a surface. For example, when sound hits a wall, it is reflected and an echo is heard.

retina: the light-sensitive layer at the back of the eye. Light is received by the retina, which sends signals to the brain to be processed in order to understand what is being seen by the eye.

GLOSSARY

solid: a state of matter. Solids have a fixed shape and volume. The particles in solids are packed together more tightly than they are in liquids and gases.

sound: anything that can be heard by the human (or animal) ear.

sound-wave: a type of vibration that travels through a medium (solid, liquid or gas) and carries sound from one location to another.

surface area: the amount of space that covers the outside of a three dimensional object. For example, on a cube, the surface area is the total amount of area that the six faces of the cube cover. Depending on the size of the object, it's usually measured in centimetres or metres squared (cm2 or m2).

texture: how something feels when you touch it. For example, an object may have a rough or smooth texture.

translucent: objects or materials that some light can pass through, but not all of it. Looking through a translucent object or material will make the view appear blurry.

transparent: objects or material that allows light to pass through without being blocked. Items viewed through a transparent material or object will be seen clearly.

transverse wave: a type of wave where the particles in the medium (solid, liquid or gas) move up and down (or side to side). The particles move at right angles to the direction they're travelling in.

tungsten: the strongest metal in the world. It has the highest melting point of any metal at 3,422 ° Celsius.

GLOSSARY

vacuum: a space where there is no matter whatsoever. A vacuum has no air particles in it, so no sound or heat can be carried as they require a medium.

Van de Graaff generator: a machine that creates a high voltage by building up static electricity. Electrons are transferred from one object to another, which builds up a high electrical charge in the metal sphere.

volts: the measurement of how much strength the electrical current in a circuit is pushed with. The harder the electrical current is pushed, the higher the voltage.

wavelength: the distance from one peak (highest point) of a wave to the next peak. It tells you how long or short a wave is. Long waves have a longer distance between each peak than shorter waves.